"*The Self-Esteem Workbook for Teens* is outstanding and very needed. Every chapter made me think of a teen who would benefit from this. I love the affirmations in each chapter. This workbook has so many valuable messages and activities to help teens build up their self-esteem. Another inspiring winner for this school social worker to utilize."

—**Ellen Griffith, MSW**, middle school social worker

T0048973

"I've used Lisa Schab's workbooks for teens for many years in my work with 7-12 grade students as a school counselor. I appreciate the tools and activities in this workbook because they are user-friendly, developmentally appropriate, engaging, and I see results when students take advantage of the exercises. This is a must-have resource in every school counselor's office, and a book I can refer parents to when they're looking to help their teens as well!"

—**Chelsea Roberts, BS**, Eau Claire M.S. school counseling; University of
Wisconsin – Stout; 7-12 grade school counselor at Gibraltar Secondary School

"This is a warm and wonderfully written workbook! It will not only guide teens to wholesome self-esteem, but will also help them through the inevitable ups and downs of their lives with sound mental health. I heartily recommend it."

—**Glenn R. Schiraldi, PhD**, University of Maryland School of Public
Health (ret.), and author of *The Self-Esteem Workbook* and *The Adverse
Childhood Experiences Recovery Workbook*

"An amazing resource—everything you want in a self-esteem workbook, plus more! Practical skills and tools are framed in an inviting and engaging way, updated for today's modern world. This is a must-have on every clinician's bookshelf, and a true gift for parents and teens alike who are looking for accessible support."

—**Cheryl M. Bradshaw, RP, MA**, author of *The Resilience Workbook for Teens*
and *How to Like Yourself*

"Bolstering authentic self-esteem is critical to self-acceptance and mental well-being. *The Self-Esteem Workbook for Teens* offers teens, parents, and adults who work with them an engaging and effective tool. Relevant scenarios give teens an understanding of what self-esteem is based on, and activities allow them to explore their beliefs and interests to recognize and appreciate their strengths. Daily affirmations are helpful in highlighting the essential concepts."

—**Mary K. Alvord, PhD**, psychologist, and coauthor of *Conquer Negative Thinking for Teens* and *Resilience Builder Program for Children and Adolescents*

"Yet another excellent workbook for teens by Lisa M. Schab! *The Self Esteem Workbook for Teens* is a useful tool that actively engages teens utilizing enjoyable and introspective activities to help them explore ways to build positive self-esteem. Teens, parents, therapists, and anyone who works with teens would find this book to be an incredible resource to include in their library."

—**Ariel Callen, BS**, certified family-based therapist

"Lisa Schab's workbook provides the reader with excellent tools to better understand themselves, where they are, and where they want to go. With this deeper understanding, they can embrace their whole selves and live a more authentic, fulfilling, and successful life."

—**Michelle Skeen, PsyD**, author of *Just As You Are* and *Love Me Don't Leave Me*

"*The Self-Esteem Workbook for Teens* is essential to have in a social-emotional learning tool kit. The workbook is an invaluable resource for teens and professionals which provides guided lessons and practical activities to explore self-acceptance, and teaches positive skills to encourage personal growth during the challenging journey of adolescence. The expanded activities in this edition offer further opportunities for self-discovery, self-reflection, and building positive and healthy relationships."

—**Jenny Szewczyk, NCSP**, school psychologist at Westbrook High School in Westbrook, CT

Praise for the 1st Edition:

"This is a brilliant, inspiring book that teaches and guides teens to navigate their inner world, as well as the world they live in. In a masterful piece, Schab has encompassed all aspects of teenagers' experience: body, mind, spirit, and relationships. The workbook format offers results-oriented lessons for a lifetime of healthy self-esteem. I highly recommend this book to anyone who has a teenager or has ever been one."

> —**Susan Schwass, LCSW**, private practitioner working with teens and their families for thirty-five years

"*The Self-Esteem Workbook for Teens* actively engages students in a gentle self-exploration of the ways both internal and external factors influence their self-perceptions and well-being. The workbook is set up with a logical flow that provides information, engages the student in thoughtful self-analysis, and offers reflection on one's individual strengths and positive attributes. Additionally, the workbook guides students in changing behaviors and thought processes detrimental to their well-being. The scenarios in the book provide relatable, real-life situations of which the adolescent can easily make sense."

> —**Wendy Merryman, PhD**, counselor in the Central Dauphin School District, working to promote positive personal, social, emotional, and academic growth of students in individual, small-group, and classroom settings

"This book offers teenagers empathetic, honest, and clear ways to challenge self-esteem and build self-insight. It touches on everything from society's external, often overbearing mixed messages—which teenagers encounter daily—to deep, personal internal conflicts and family dynamics. The numerous, unique activities offer teens a safe and positive space to change their thoughts and actions, ultimately helping them to have more successful relationships and high school careers."

> —**Nicole Brown, MAAT, LPC, CYI**, the Child, Adolescent, and Family Recovery Center; and the Child, Adolescent, and Family Development Center

"Lisa Schab's workbook on self-esteem for teens is replete with commonsense exercises and instructions that are all informed by current research and developmental theory. Each of the 'Know This' prefaces illustrate Schab's practical wisdom and advanced clinical skills as a psychotherapist and professional whose knowledge spans the emotions, minds, and behaviors of both teens and their families."

—**Randolph Lucente, PhD**, professor of adolescent psychology at
Loyola University Chicago's School of Social Work

"*The Self-Esteem Workbook for Teens* provides a comprehensive, usable format of step-by-step progression toward a healthy self-concept—the foundation of effective learning. Lisa Schab has developed a program designed to encourage self-reflection, self-awareness, perseverance, and the importance of taking action to improve the situation. Throughout, teens are counseled to pay attention to and act upon the urgings of the authentic self—an incredibly valuable life skill. The workbook could easily be used by either individuals or groups."

—**Nancy Hanrahan, MA, NCC**, school counselor at St. Joseph School
in Libertyville, IL

"Adolescence is often a bewildering time when self-esteem gets battered. Teens regularly second-guess themselves and worry about their self-worth, leading them to engage in self-destructive behaviors. This workbook gives readers practical, creative, and empowering tools to not only explore their identity, but build self-confidence and make smart, healthy decisions. It also helps teens become critical consumers, discover their passions, navigate peer pressure, and become more compassionate toward themselves and others. It's truly a must-read for any teen!"

—**Margarita Tartakovsky, MS**, associate editor at www.psychcentral.com

"This workbook encompasses all aspects of a teen's journey to a higher self-esteem."

—**Tracey Engdahl**, juvenile corrections counselor

the self-esteem workbook for teens

SECOND EDITION

activities to help you build confidence & achieve your goals

LISA M. SCHAB, LCSW

Instant Help Books
An Imprint of New Harbinger Publications, Inc.

INSTANT HELP, the Clock Logo, and NEW HARBINGER are trademarks of New Harbinger Publications, Inc.

New Harbinger Publications is an employee-owned company.

Distributed in Canada by Raincoast Books

Copyright © 2022 by Lisa Schab
        Instant Help Books
        An imprint of New Harbinger Publications, Inc.
        5674 Shattuck Avenue
        Oakland, CA 94609
        www.newharbinger.com

All Rights Reserved

Cover design by Amy Shoup

Acquired by Tesilya Hanauer

Edited by Karen Schader

FSC
www.fsc.org
MIX
Paper from
responsible sources
FSC® C011935

Library of Congress Cataloging-in-Publication Data on file

Printed in the United States of America

25   24   23

10   9   8   7   6   5   4   3

Contents

Dear Reader,

Welcome to the first page of an important journey—the journey to yourself! In this book you'll find activities that will help you get to know who you are, understand how you came to be that person, and explore who you still want to become. You'll be presented with the concept of self-worth and asked to believe that you have just as much worth as any other person on this planet.

Some of the activities will help you understand what outside factors affect your thoughts, feelings, and behaviors. Others will help you explore who you are at your core—your authentic self—before you're influenced by anyone or anything else.

You'll learn ways to stay true to your authentic self even when faced with outside pressures. You'll acquire a significant number of tools to help you make your way through your life successfully, realizing positive outcomes through the thoughts you think and the choices you make. Some of these tools are available for download at the website for this book: http://www.newharbinger.com/50003.

An underlying premise of this book is: *You're okay just the way you are!* This is a basic tenet of healthy self-esteem: that we accept ourselves unconditionally—weaknesses, strengths, everything—no matter what. Some activities will help you work on this concept. Others will help you identify and focus on your strengths so you have something to celebrate on the days when it's hard to believe that you really are okay.

Accepting every part of ourselves doesn't mean we don't try to improve or grow. You'll also find activities that teach you how to gain inner strength, handle challenges and relationships better, and achieve your goals. Reading and repeating the affirmations at the end of each activity will help the concepts become real for you.

My hope is that you'll learn to understand, accept, and embrace the truth of your inherent value as a human being. Because when you actually comprehend your equality to all other beings, you can open yourself to your own love and acceptance. And that is the foundation of healthy self-esteem.

Whatever you are feeling right now, know that you have the courage to begin this amazing journey. Be open to the adventure. I wish you the very best!

—Lisa M. Schab, LCSW

to parents, professionals, and all helping adults

Recognition…

The first edition of *The Self-Esteem Workbook for Teens* (2013) has been translated into eight foreign languages and is recognized around the world as a leading resource for building self-esteem in teens. In 2018 it was named one of Tutorful's best child self-esteem resources and is continually recommended on mental health websites for professionals, parents, and teens.

The purpose of this workbook is to help teens—both those at risk and those simply traveling through an average adolescence—to develop or enhance a state of healthy self-esteem, meaning a positive regard for oneself, and including an understanding and acceptance of one's weaknesses; a celebration of one's strengths; and a realistic conviction of one's equality to others.

Teens with healthy self-esteem are able to know and accept themselves, practice compassion for both self and others, act with integrity and self-discipline, and use healthy coping skills, both cognitively and behaviorally, to meet life challenges. They are convinced of their unconditional worth despite changing external circumstances, and they are also convinced of and respect the worth of others.

The activities in this book are designed to help adolescents explore, understand, and value their authentic and unique selves and to teach them skills that will enable them to mature and move down their own paths with confidence, integrity, and peace.

Second Edition: Same solid base plus sixteen new activities…

New activities in the second edition also address issues and skills that help teens develop healthy relationships, success and achievement, and a positive self-image. Topics include:

- Releasing devaluing messages
- Managing social media

- Body image issues (two activities)
- Celebrating strengths and working with weaknesses
- Assertive communication
- Basic social skills
- Setting healthy boundaries
- Not taking things personally
- Tolerating people not liking you
- Healthy thinking habits
- Problem-solving skills
- Turning around negative life choices
- Developing inner peace
- The look of healthy self-esteem
- Asking for help

Meeting counseling, social-emotional learning (SEL) and trauma-informed classroom needs...

Not only can teens use *The Self-Esteem Workbook* on their own as self-help, but therapists, social workers, and counselors will continue to find it an invaluable resource for use with both individual clients and groups. Educators and school staff will find practical, easy-to-understand-and-implement worksheets that address core SEL and trauma topics.

Thank you so much for your dedication to the teens in your life. May you both benefit from working through this book together!

—Lisa M. Schab, LCSW

know this

Having healthy self-esteem means you have a strong sense of self-worth. You understand and accept your weaknesses, and you appreciate and celebrate your strengths. When you have healthy self-esteem, you recognize the inborn value of all people, including yourself.

Very basically, self-esteem is how you feel about yourself. If you want to feel truthfully good about yourself down at the deepest level, you need healthy self-esteem.

People with healthy self-esteem generally have positive thoughts and feelings about themselves. They are certain enough of their equality with others that they can admit their faults without feeling ashamed and enjoy their strengths without putting others down. People without healthy self-esteem generally have negative thoughts and feelings about themselves. They aren't confident in their equality to others, so they feel ashamed when they make mistakes and may put others down in order to cover up their insecurity.

Healthy self-esteem is a deep knowing that you are a valuable person (and so is everyone else!). When you understand this, you don't need to have someone else affirm you or achieve a certain goal to feel good about yourself. You don't have to feel better than someone else to know you're okay. You know your self-worth doesn't depend on whether you win or lose.

Thoughts like these come from healthy self-esteem:

I'll just keep trying until I get it.

I can tell she doesn't like me, but that's okay.

I love wearing this shirt even though it's not in style.

It's all right if we disagree.

I didn't win, but even placing is awesome.

Thoughts like these come from unhealthy self-esteem:

I have to make the team so I can prove I'm as good as them.

I feel so stupid when I make mistakes.

They're probably lying; it's hard to trust anyone.

I'm always second best.

I hate this school; everyone's conceited.

How you feel about yourself is one of the most significant factors in how you'll experience every aspect of your life, including classes, parties, dating relationships, job interviews, and the family dinner table. When you have healthy self-esteem, you have a better chance at success and happiness in everything you do.

try this

For each of the following conversations check the reply you think illustrates the healthiest self-esteem:

Congratulations on winning the freestyle swim relay!

☐ "Thanks, it feels good. And you won the diving competition—that's great!"

☐ "I don't know why I won. I don't have good form."

☐ "Yeah, I made those other swimmers look like tadpoles!"

I hear Benjamin broke up with you. How are you feeling?

☐ "Couldn't be better. I was planning to dump him anyway. He was dragging me down."

☐ "I figured it would happen. No one sticks with me once they get to know me."

☐ "I was pretty sad for a while, but I'm better now."

"Excuse me, but I think you're in the wrong seat. Could you check your ticket?"

☐ "Oh, sorry! I always mess things up!"

☐ "Excuse me, but I was here first. Why don't you find an empty seat?"

☐ "You're right; I apologize. I'm supposed to be in the row behind."

Hey, that's my sweater. You didn't ask if you could borrow it!

☐ "Sorry. You weren't home, but I should have asked you first."

☐ "Quit whining. It looks better on me anyway."

☐ "I don't know what I was thinking. It doesn't even look good on me. I'll give you one of mine to make up for it."

now try this

Teens who have healthy self-esteem generally

_____ know and accept themselves;

_____ practice compassion for themselves and others;

_____ act with integrity and self-discipline;

_____ use healthy coping skills in their thoughts and actions to meet life challenges;

_____ keep a conviction of their unconditional worth despite changing circumstances;

_____ choose and stand by their own thoughts, feelings, and behaviors, instead of giving in to pressure from others;

_____ remain convinced of and act with respect for the worth of others.

Put a star next to the above characteristics that you already do well.

Rewrite the characteristics you still need to work on below:

_____

_____

_____

_____

_____

_____

_____

Tell how working on healthy self-esteem could help you personally in the following areas:

Friends _____

_____

Family _____

_____

School _____

_____

Dating _____

_____

Work _____

_____

Describe one or two specific self-esteem goals you'd like to work toward as you go through this book:

_____

_____

_____

today's affirmation

I recognize and affirm my equality to others and their equality to me.

2 recognize your power: your self-esteem is in your hands

know this

When we believe that other people or external circumstances control our self-esteem, we make ourselves victims—dependent on something outside ourselves to feel okay. In reality, no matter what anyone else thinks or what happens to us, only *we* decide how to think about ourselves. When we embrace this power, we can create healthy self-esteem at any moment.

Jonna was diagnosed with attention deficit/hyperactivity disorder, or ADHD. This meant the way her brain worked made it harder for her to focus on certain things. Jonna's cousin, Mason, said, "That's weird. I don't know anyone who has that. You're going to have a hard time in school—and in everything!" Jonna could listen to what Mason said and think, He's right, I'm weird. I'll probably lose my friends when they find out. I might not pass my classes either; it'll be so embarrassing. How can I face people? *Or she could listen to what Mason said and think,* Mason doesn't know much about ADHD; it's a pretty common disorder. I'll need some help at first, but lots of people need help with things. It doesn't make me weird. *Mason can't choose Jonna's thoughts for her; only Jonna can decide what she thinks about herself.*

Ava blamed her father for her low self-esteem. When she was little, he left and never came back. She always wondered if it was because he didn't like her or she wasn't good enough. When she thought this way, she'd feel bad about herself. One day Ava realized her self-esteem could never change as long as she based it on this fictional story. She might never know how her father felt about her but she didn't have to spend the rest of her life feeling down on herself. She decided to let go of this negative thinking, take back her power, and remember that her self-esteem was in her hands, not her father's.

try this

Circle any of the following items that you think prevent you from having healthy self-esteem. Write more of your own on the lines below.

parents	divorce	physical handicaps
friends	abuse	family history
teachers	learning disabilities	_____
relatives	finances	_____
strangers	emotional handicaps	_____

Which of these items have you blamed the most for hurting your self-esteem?

_____

_____

What does it feel like to think about taking your power back and putting your self-esteem in your own hands?

_____

_____

What would be the hardest part of doing this?

_____

_____

What would be the best part of doing this?

_____

_____

now try this

Write the thoughts Jonna chose to take back her self-esteem from Mason.

_____

_____

_____

_____

_____

Write the thoughts Ava chose to take back her self-esteem from her father.

_____

_____

_____

_____

_____

What thoughts can you choose to change from blaming something outside yourself to taking charge of your own self-esteem?

_____

_____

_____

_____

_____

Trace your hand here. All across the shape write about how you're going to put your self-esteem into your own hands. It might be hard, but this book will help you gain the strength, skills, and thinking habits that will empower you to do it.

today's affirmation

I am not a victim. My self-esteem is in my hands.

3 claim your intrinsic value and worth

know this

Every human being who ever lived came into this world with value and worth. There has never been an exception. This includes you.

Everyone arrives on this planet as an amazing spark of life with the same intrinsic value and worth. Every infant is equally significant; each has value; each is a miracle. You are one of those miracles. No matter where you were born, what the circumstances of your birth were, or whom you were born to, you arrived with value. And just like every other person, you still have it. It doesn't matter what you've said or done or been told—you came in with value and you'll have it the rest of your life. Nothing can change that.

As you grew you may have received and believed messages that caused you to think otherwise. Maybe your hair is straight and someone said wavy is "better." Maybe you love to write poetry and someone said writing poetry is "silly." Maybe you made a mistake and someone said you're "bad." Maybe your caregivers ignored you and you think you're not worthy of attention.

It's essential to remember that nothing can change your intrinsic value. You might make mistakes, be abandoned, get into trouble, or be criticized, but these don't change your innate value and worth. Remembering this truth is a basic foundation for healthy self-esteem.

try this

Think about any newborn baby you've ever met. If you don't know any, imagine one. Imagine that tiny child, newly arrived, taking its first breaths, completely helpless and dependent on its caregivers. Think about the miracle of its birth, and think about its innocence. Check any of the statements that a medical professional might tell this baby's parents.

- ☐ "This baby isn't as good as the others."

- ☐ "It appears this child has no value."

- ☐ "You've created a human being with no worth."

- ☐ "This infant has absolutely no potential."

- ☐ "This child is wrong."

- ☐ "Your baby appears to be worthless."

It might sound absurd to think of a doctor making any of these claims about a child. And it is. It is just as absurd to think any of these statements about yourself. You were that newborn infant at one time, and your value has not disappeared over time.

In the frame below, draw or paste a picture of yourself as a newborn. Write your full name on the line underneath.

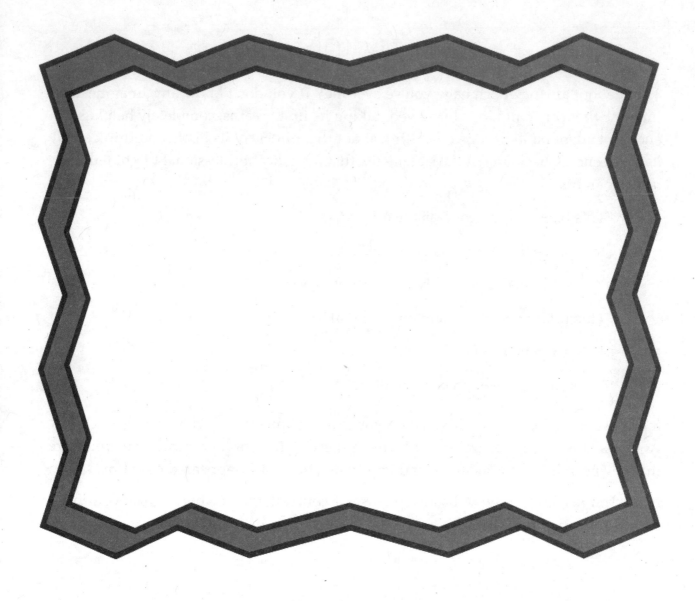

Copy this statement: "Unconditional, intrinsic human worth exists constantly despite changing achievements, failures, or external circumstances."

_____

_____

_____

now try this

List situations in which you have thought of yourself as worthless or flawed.

_____

_____

_____

_____

Write what you told yourself at these times.

_____

_____

_____

_____

Give any factual, verifiable information that could confirm that you actually have no value; for example, this was printed on your birth certificate, and you have a copy of it.

_____

_____

_____

_____

Tell why you think you have come to believe that you are worthless or flawed.

_____

_____

_____

_____

Using your own words, write a commitment to yourself to stop believing that lie.

_____

_____

_____

_____

_____

today's affirmation

I have the same innate value and worth as every
other person born into this world.

release devaluing messages 4

know this

When we're young we receive lots of messages that affect how we feel about ourselves. These messages may come from family members, other people, or the society or culture we live in. When we're aware of the messages and how they affect us, we can make a choice to release those that devalue us and negatively affect our self-esteem.

Dion's mom suffered from depression and alcohol abuse and never got the help she needed. She had a low stress tolerance and often blamed Dion for her problems, saying it was his fault she struggled so much in life. This wasn't true, but she wasn't healthy enough to see the real origin of her troubles. Dion grew up thinking, I made my mom sick; I make people feel bad; and I'm not good enough, *A high school counselor finally explained to Dion that his mom's struggles were present long before he was born. Although he hadn't caused them, believing that devaluing message was hurting his self-esteem.*

Logan grew up watching sports with his family. Sometimes he and his dad went to sporting events or ate at restaurants owned by famous athletes. Logan learned indirectly that his culture valued athletes. But Logan wasn't athletic and had no interest in joining either team or individual sports. He had a solid group of friends who enjoyed working on computers and excelled in computer science. But Logan still held himself up to the social message that "being athletic is good," and always felt like he fell short of what was "right." Believing this message damaged his self-esteem.

Lily's dad was always trying to motivate her. He hadn't been encouraged by his own parents and wanted to do better for Lily. Whenever Lily accomplished something, her dad would praise her and then say, "Now let's see if you can do even better next time!" Lily's dad was proud of himself for trying to instill drive and hope into his daughter. But Lily didn't hear his message that way. Lily grew up thinking she was never good enough because no matter how much she accomplished her dad always wanted more. Lily's understanding of her dad's message was very different from what he intended.

Hailey went to a private high school where most students planned to go to college and graduate school after that. Hailey got excellent grades but knew she didn't want an advanced degree. She was very creative and wanted to be a weaver like her grandmother. She'd already designed her own patterns and won competitions at art shows. But Hailey's teachers were always encouraging her to look into other fields. Hailey got the indirect message that there was something wrong with her because she didn't want to go to college.

try this

Underline any of the following messages family members may have sent you, either directly or indirectly.

Wow, you're really good at that.

You're not trying hard enough.

I was so happy when you were born.

You'll never be able to do that.

Why can't you be more like your brother/sister?

I'm so proud of you.

You are an awesome person.

You drive me crazy.

When are you going to grow up?

You can succeed at anything you want to.

Are you stupid or something?

It's great that you follow your own path.

How will you ever get anywhere in life?

I have so much confidence in you.

Can't you do anything right?

I knew you could do it.

List any other family messages you hear in your head that affect your self-esteem but are not included above.

_____

_____

_____

_____

_____

_____

_____

_____

Put a star by the messages that help you feel good about yourself.

Put a D by the messages that feel devaluing to you.

On a separate piece of paper, rewrite the messages that devalue you and then take a step to release them from your mind. Put the words through a shredder or rip them up and throw them away. Remind yourself that you have a choice about which messages you continue to tell yourself.

now try this

We receive social messages through media such as radio, television, internet, movies, and magazines. We also receive them from individuals such as parents, politicians, teachers, faith leaders, writers, lobbyists, experts, business spokespeople, and celebrities.

We receive messages directly when people talk openly to us, like when a rep from the Environmental Protection Agency promotes recycling at a school assembly. We receive messages indirectly through channels such as commercials for preventing child abuse, advertisements claiming the best way to look, and billboards promoting certain religious beliefs.

Over the next week, record the social messages you receive from any of the above sources or others. Record whether you agree or disagree with the message. Then record how the message has affected your self-esteem. Draw an upward pointing arrow if it raises your self-esteem, a downward pointing arrow if it lowers your self-esteem, or a straight line if it doesn't affect your self-esteem at all.

Social message	Source	Agree or disagree	Effect on self-esteem

Look back at your chart and describe any patterns you notice.

_____

_____

_____

_____

List any of the messages you'd like to release.

_____

_____

_____

_____

Rewrite these messages on a separate piece of paper and then put the words through a shredder or rip them up and throw them away. Tell how it felt to destroy these devaluing messages.

today's affirmation

I can let go of any messages that don't contribute
to my healthy self-esteem.

5 choose positive self-messages

know this

The way you feel about yourself today is partly due to the messages you send yourself. These messages help you feel good or bad about yourself. When you identify, explore, and evaluate your self-messages, you can decide which you want to keep and which you don't. You can learn new ways to talk to yourself that help you develop healthy self-esteem.

Whether or not you open your mouth to speak, you actually "talk" to yourself all day long. There is a running dialogue inside your head, an inner voice sending you messages that affect how you feel about yourself.

I shouldn't have said that…That was an awesome movie…I really like her…He's so rude…I hate this class…I can't believe I failed again…This tastes awful. The messages go on and on. Those that we tell about ourselves help create our self-esteem.

When Camila makes a mistake in a band concert, she tells herself, I wish I hadn't done that, but I improved overall and that's awesome! *When she doesn't have a date for the dance, she tells herself,* I still have great friends to spend the night with. *Her positive self-messages help create healthy self-esteem.*

When Caleb makes a mistake in a band concert, he tells himself, I messed up again, I'll never be good at this. *When he doesn't have a date for the dance, he tells himself,* No one will ever go out with me, I'm such a loser. *His negative self-messages help create unhealthy self-esteem.*

You've been telling yourself messages since you were a young child, although you weren't necessarily aware of them. As a young adult, you now have the ability to explore and pay attention to those messages. Then you can decide which to keep and which to let go of.

try this

Think about the messages you've sent yourself throughout the course of your life. If you can't remember exactly, take a guess. What did you tell yourself when you:

Fell off your bike when you were first learning to ride?

_____

Had a hard time learning something in school?

_____

Were rejected by a friend?

_____

Didn't get the ball through the basketball hoop?

_____

Were reprimanded by your parents?

_____

Made a mistake?

_____

Weren't picked first for a team?

_____

Over the next few days, listen for your self-messages. Notice the responses you give yourself to situations that occur throughout the day. Record your messages in the chart below (or download a copy at http://www.newharbinger.com/50003), keeping track of how many times you use them, and circle whether they make your self-esteem go up, go down, or stay the same.

Self-message	Number of times used	Self-esteem		
		Up	Down	Same
		Up	Down	Same
		Up	Down	Same
		Up	Down	Same
		Up	Down	Same
		Up	Down	Same
		Up	Down	Same
		Up	Down	Same
		Up	Down	Same

Circle any of these words that describe your self-messages. Use the blank lines to add your own words.

positive	compassionate	irrational	unfair
harsh	caring	considerate	_____
kind	negative	gentle	_____
rational	fair	offensive	_____
demeaning	rude	loving	_____

How do your self-messages compare to the messages you would send to a friend?

better   the same   worse

now try this

Imagine you are the best parent in the world and you are taking care of yourself as a little child. On the lines below, make a list of positive, loving messages you would want to tell yourself as you're growing up. Think about what you needed and wanted to hear as a child. It may have been something like "You are an awesome kid," "I love you so much," "You are skilled and talented," "I love and accept you unconditionally," or "I'm so glad you're my child."

_____

_____

_____

_____

_____

_____

Next, make a list of the positive and loving messages you need and want to hear right now as a teen. Maybe these sound like, "I'm so proud of you," "It's okay if your grades aren't perfect," "I love and accept you just the way you are," and so on.

_____

_____

_____

_____

_____

_____

Remember, you create your own self-esteem so when you send yourself these positive messages, you will reap their benefits. Make a commitment to read your positive self-messages every day as many times as you're able until you have them memorized. You can also try:

Saying them out loud in front of a mirror.

Sending them to yourself in a text.

Sending them to yourself in an email.

Writing them on sticky notes and posting them where you'll see them frequently.

Writing them in your assignment book.

Or...(add your own ideas)

_____

_____

_____

_____

_____

When you instill these positive self-messages in your mind, they'll eventually start appearing automatically whenever you feel disappointed, discouraged, or down on yourself. Using them over and over will help you build healthy self-esteem.

today's affirmation

I choose self-messages that create healthy self-esteem.

know this

Compassion means a deep sympathy or caring. Being able to feel compassion for every human being, including yourself, is a cornerstone of healthy self-esteem.

We have all been born and we will all die. We all want to succeed and we all want to feel happy. We all want to feel good about ourselves and we all want to feel loved. We all struggle to survive in a way that will bring us the most peace and the least pain. We are all doing the best we can with what we have.

On the most basic level, everyone is made from the same essential stuff—physically, emotionally, and spiritually. We are all in this life experience together, on an even playing field. No one is greater than—or less than—anyone else. Realizing the ways we are alike and the basic drives and instincts we all share brings us the gift of compassion.

Compassion arises when we no longer feel insecure about ourselves. We can feel compassion for others when we no longer feel threatened by them. We can feel compassion for ourselves when we accept our human condition—our strengths and our flaws—and when we love and accept ourselves no matter what. Compassion for every living creature helps us achieve healthy self-esteem.

try this

Record the level of concern or sympathy you would feel for each of the following people or animals on a scale of 1 (low) to 10 (high) and then record the feeling or feelings you experience. Choose your feelings from the following list or write your own.

pain   sadness   helplessness   anger

1. your friend whose parent has died

   Concern/sympathy: _____   Feeling(s): _____

2. a puppy limping in the street in the rain

   Concern/sympathy: _____   Feeling(s): _____

3. a person on the news who lost everything in a hurricane

   Concern/sympathy: _____   Feeling(s): _____

4. a child who has a terminal illness

   Concern/sympathy: _____   Feeling(s): _____

5. your grandparent who is aging

   Concern/sympathy: _____   Feeling(s): _____

6. your younger sibling who was harshly punished by your parents

   Concern/sympathy: _____   Feeling(s): _____

7. a blind kitten

   Concern/sympathy: _____   Feeling(s): _____

8. a homeless person you see on the street

   Concern/sympathy: _____   Feeling(s): _____

9. someone on the side of the highway whose car has broken down

    Concern/sympathy: _____   Feeling(s): _____

10. farm animals who have been physically abused

    Concern/sympathy: _____   Feeling(s): _____

Check any of the following statements you might use when you are speaking with compassion.

☐ I'm sorry this happened to you.

☐ How can I help?

☐ Are you okay?

☐ Tell me what I can do.

☐ I want to help.

☐ It will be okay.

☐ I will help you through this.

☐ I care about you.

☐ It will get better.

☐ Other: _____

Circle any of these compassionate actions you are comfortable doing:

listening   giving time

hugging   giving emotional support

giving energy   giving financial support

paying attention   other: _____

Choose two of the above situations and tell how you would treat that person or animal with compassion.

Situation number _____

What I would say: _____

_____

What I would do: _____

_____

Situation number _____

What I would say: _____

_____

What I would do: _____

_____

now try this

You may not be used to directing compassion toward yourself, but if you know how to treat others with compassion, you also know how to treat yourself. Think about the compassionate words and actions listed above, and describe how you could show compassion for yourself in the following situations.

Someone you'd like to date tells you they're not interested.

_____

You forget the words to your chorus solo.

_____

You don't make the team.

_____

You feel lonely.

_____

You give the wrong answer when the teacher calls on you.

_____

You've had a rough day.

_____

Think of a struggle you've been experiencing recently. On a separate sheet of paper, write a compassionate letter to yourself with regard to this. Use the words and feelings you might use to show compassion to your best friend.

today's affirmation

Treating myself with compassion is an act of healthy self-esteem.

7 the perfection of diversity

know this

You are genetically programmed to be yourself—and only yourself. This means you can be successful only by following your own path and becoming the best possible you.

When we aren't happy with ourselves, we may look at other people and wish we were like them. We might even try to become more like them. When we do this, we set ourselves up to fail. One human being can no more become another than an eagle can become a flamingo or a towering evergreen can become an oak.

The natural state of the universe is variety and diversity. The multitudes of species of trees, insects, birds, flowers, and animals all confirm this truth. Likewise, there are different shapes, sizes, and colors of human beings. This rich diversity exists for a purpose. There are supposed to be differences between us so that every task in nature gets accomplished. There are supposed to be different kinds of plant life and animal life—and human life.

Each individual human being is a unique combination of cells, genes, ideas, feelings, talents, and skills. To be successful in life, we must recognize, celebrate, and follow our own unique paths. Even if we devote all our energy to trying to become someone else—perhaps someone we think is "better" than us—we will only fail. Only when we try to be our own best selves can we find healthy self-esteem.

try this

Describe what might happen if there were only one type of plant in the world.

_____

_____

Describe what might happen if there were only one type of animal.

_____

_____

Think of someone you sometimes wish you were. If you spent every ounce of your energy for every day of your life trying to become that person, could you succeed?

_____

_____

What would happen in the world if everyone had the same set of talents and skills?

_____

_____

What would happen if everyone had the same job?

_____

_____

What would happen if everyone looked alike?

_____

_____

now try this

Draw a scene from an imagined world where all life forms are alike. Include plants, animals, humans, insects, or whatever you like. Remember to make all forms in each category look alike.

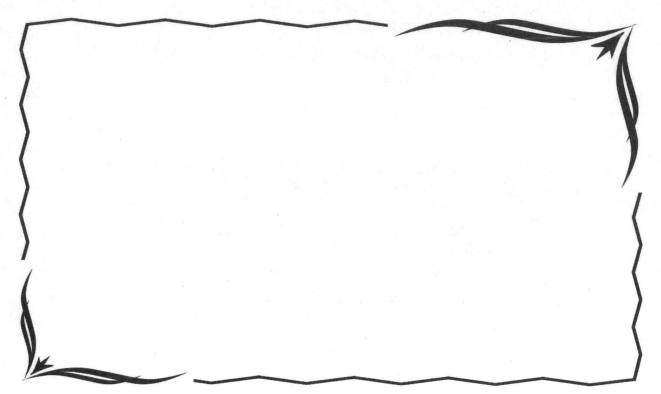

Look at your picture, and describe your thoughts and feelings about a world like this.

_____

_____

_____

Now draw a scene from your personal real world, but draw it *without* diversity. For example, maybe in real life you have a mellow black Lab and an energetic terrier as pets. In your picture, both your pets would have to be the same. In real life, you might have an athletic friend you enjoy sports with and another friend with a great sense of humor whom you love watching movies with. In your picture, both your friends would have to be the same.

Look at this picture, and describe your thoughts and feelings about a world like this.

_____

_____

_____

today's affirmation

Being myself celebrates the world's natural state of diversity and creates success and healthy self–esteem.

8 your authentic self is your best self

know this

Your authentic self is who you are before you change things—thoughts, feelings, looks, or actions—because you think you have to. It's who you are before you're affected by external expectations or opinions. Many of us have lost track of our authentic selves because we've tried so hard to be something else. The healthier our self-esteem, the better we can know, trust, and express our authentic selves.

Isabella's girlfriends were so into horses that they took riding lessons twice a week and volunteered at the stables in their free time. Isabella really had no interest in horses but she pretended to like them because her friends did. She asked for riding boots for her birthday, took lessons after school, and spent her free time at the stables.

One day while Isabella was grooming a horse, the stable owner, Vivie, said, "You look like your mind is a million miles away! What are you thinking about?"

"Running," said Isabella. "Sign-ups for the cross-country team are today. I love running. I've always wanted to be on the team."

"Then what on earth are you doing here?" asked Vivie.

"Well, my friends are here. And I like to be with them. And it's cool to like horses..."

"It sounds like you're here because of what other people want, not what you want," said Vivie. "You're not acting from your authentic self. How do you feel when you run, and how do you feel when you're here?"

"When I run, I feel fantastic," said Isabella. "It might sound funny, but I feel at home, like I was born to run. When I'm here, I feel...kind of out of place...like I'm just visiting."

"That's because you are," said Vivie. "You're visiting your friends' lives. I suggest you go back to your own life and get on that team. Listen to your authentic self and start running!"

try this

Very young children are usually still in touch with their authentic selves. They haven't yet been influenced by other people's opinions. Describe anything you can remember about what you liked to do, what you liked to play with, or whom you liked to spend time with when you were a child.

_____

_____

_____

_____

List the elective activities you are involved in now. Rate each activity from 1 (low) to 10 (high) according to how much your authentic self wants to do it. Next to your rating, explain why you are doing it, if not for your authentic self.

Activity	AS rating	Why I'm doing this

Circle the AS below next to any choice you make from your authentic self. Circle the OF next to any you make because of other factors. Next to each OF choice, write what those factors are; for example, "My parents make me"; "I want to fit in"; "It's against the rules"; "We can't afford what I really want"; "It's cool."

AS   OF   What I wear _____

AS   OF   What music I listen to _____

AS   OF   What I eat for lunch _____

AS   OF   What I do on weekends _____

AS   OF   Who my friends are _____

AS   OF   What I do during the summer _____

AS   OF   What I read _____

AS   OF   How I use social media _____

AS   OF   How I spend my money _____

Describe what you would do differently regarding these activities if you were acting only from your authentic self.

_____

_____

_____

_____

_____

_____

now try this

Place a check mark next to any of these words that you think describes you. Then circle those that describe you when you are being your authentic self. (You may both check and circle the same words.) Use the blank lines to add your own words.

☐ assertive	☐ anxious	☐ compassionate	☐ incompetent
☐ needy	☐ clumsy	☐ quiet	☐ dishonest
☐ calm	☐ conceited	☐ cruel	☐ responsible
☐ promiscuous	☐ rude	☐ well-behaved	☐ reliable
☐ honest	☐ busy	☐ lazy	☐ joyful
☐ thoughtful	☐ loving	☐ talkative	☐ discouraged
☐ sad	☐ bored	☐ studious	☐ sensitive
☐ kind	☐ friendly	☐ wise	☐ outgoing
☐ hardworking	☐ afraid	☐ brave	☐ passive
☐ angry	☐ creative	☐ isolated	☐ overwhelmed
☐ curious	☐ loyal	☐ conflicted	☐ healthy
☐ confused	☐ generous	☐ empty	☐ rigid
☐ athletic	☐ relaxed	☐ peaceful	_____
☐ selfish	☐ smart	☐ depressed	_____
☐ prejudiced	☐ confident	☐ aggressive	_____
☐ lonely	☐ loud	☐ flexible	_____
☐ happy	☐ accepting	☐ active	_____

How do your checks and circles compare?

_____

_____

_____

_____

What can you learn about your authentic self from this exercise?

_____

_____

_____

_____

_____

_____

_____

_____

today's affirmation

My authentic self is my best self.

who you are for your family 9

know this

Being part of a family can influence the choices you make about how you think, feel, and act. You may play a certain role in your family. You may try to live up to their expectations. You may rebel against your family members or you may try to please them. Some of these decisions might be made from your authentic self; some might not.

Maddie's parents were always arguing. Sometimes their disagreements were violent, with swearing and threats and one or both of them storming out of the house. Their fighting frightened Maddie. When she was home, she spent much of her time trying to help her parents get along, but without any success.

Ella's older brother was a star wrestler, got straight As, and was liked by everyone. Ella felt like a loser compared to him, and she started getting into trouble at school. She didn't really want to do bad things, but at least she got attention for it, which felt better than living in her brother's shadow.

Justin's mom had been struggling financially for years, and his family was often evicted for not paying rent on time. Justin's mother relied on him to have a weekend job to help pay bills, to watch his younger brothers after school, and to cook dinner when she had to work late. Justin knew his mom and brothers depended on him, and he never let them down.

Carlos had always wanted to be a teacher. He loved teaching little kids things—from bike riding to math to how to spot shooting stars. But Carlos's parents were both attorneys, and they expected him to go to law school. Carlos took political science courses to please them, but he was more interested in the tutoring he did after school.

Family situations and expectations shape our lives and help create roles for us—the parts we play in relationship to other family members—such as "achiever," "rebel," "caregiver," "clown," or "scapegoat." Even as we become more independent, family affects our choices and behaviors, our personalities, and our self-esteem. This influence can lead us to choices that are very much in line with, or very different from, our authentic selves.

41

try this

On the numbered lines below, (1) tell how you think each teen might be affected by
their family circumstances; (2) choose a role from the list below, or write your own,
that might be created by each of their situations; and (3) tell why you think this role is
or is not in line with each person's authentic self.

Maddie

1. _____
2. _____
3. _____

Ella

1. _____
2. _____
3. _____

Justin

1. _____
2. _____
3. _____

Carlos

1. _____
2. _____
3. _____

clown	intellectual	critic
disciplinarian	instigator	moralist
bully	caretaker	counselor
achiever	baby	commander-in-chief
rule keeper	rebel	loser
peacemaker	neutral party	judge
scapegoat	boss	confronter
hero	goody-goody	free spirit
overachiever	tough guy	blamer

now try this

Draw all your family members, including yourself. Add their names and the role you think each plays in your family. Choose from the list above or create your own.

Tell how it feels to play the role you play in your family.

_____

_____

Describe how you think your family expects you to:

Think _____

Talk _____

Feel _____

Behave _____

Write a number from 1 (low) to 10 (high) next to each answer above, rating how much you think you are your authentic self when you act to fill your family's expectations.

If your family had no expectations of you, tell which of the above you would do differently and which you would still do the same.

_____

_____

_____

Tell how you think your relationship with your family affects your self-esteem.

_____

_____

_____

_____

today's affirmation

Looking past the roles I play in my family helps me find my authentic self.

10 who you are for your friends

know this

Your friends can influence the choices you make about how you think, feel, and act. You may play a certain role in your peer group. You may try to live up to its expectations. You may try to fit in by pleasing your friends or identify yourself by being different. Some of these decisions might be made from your authentic self; some might not.

Mariana's best friends were Natalie and Hannah. They had known one another since kindergarten and had the best times together—at the mall or movies, on sleepovers or dates. But when she started playing co-ed volleyball, Mariana got close to Andrew and Emily. Mariana was a strong player and her new friends encouraged her. When she was with them, she focused solely on athletics and felt confident she could get a scholarship someday.

Having two sets of friends felt confusing sometimes. When she was with Natalie and Hannah, Mariana was more careful about her appearance and she talked more about boys. With Andrew and Emily she wore sweats or workout clothes, thought of herself as an athlete, and even tended to eat healthier.

Mariana liked being with both sets of friends but she began to feel like two different people.

"Which feels more like the real you?" her sister asked.

"I guess a little of each," Mariana said. "I have so much fun with Natalie and Hannah, but I also like focusing on sports with Andrew and Emily. With one group I'm the party girl; with the other I'm the athlete."

"If you change because you really like each situation, you're being true to yourself," her sister said. "But if you change because you're trying to fit in, you're just playing a game. Do what's right for you. Your true friends will stick by you no matter what."

try this

In the first column of the following chart, list one or more groups of friends to which you belong. Identify each group with a different name, such as "service club" or "neighborhood." In the next column, write the role or roles you think you play in that group. Choose from those below or write your own. In the third column rate how comfortable you feel with that group on a scale of 1 (low) to 10 (high). In last column, tell whether your self-esteem is high, average, or low when you are with that group.

Group	My role	My comfort level	Self-esteem rating
			high average low
			high average low
			high average low
			high average low
			high average low

partier	daredevil	voice of reason	peacemaker
romantic	joker	instigator	connector
listener	counselor	critic	rebel
brain	planner	bully	ghost
leader	follower	victim	speaker

now try this

Give an example of how your friends influence how you think.

_____

_____

Give an example of how your friends influence how you feel.

_____

_____

Give an example of how your friends influence how you act.

_____

_____

Describe the things you might do differently if you were not influenced by your friends.

_____

_____

On the scale below, write in each group of your friends at a point that shows how far you are from your authentic self when you are with them.

my
authentic
self

nothing at
all like my
authentic
self

today's affirmation

I choose thoughts, feelings, and actions that come from my authentic self.

who you are for society 11

know this

The society you live in can influence the choices you make about how you think, feel, and act. You may act in certain ways to feel like part of your society, or you may act in certain ways that help you feel separate from it. Some of these behaviors might come from your authentic self; some might not.

Jasmine hated her curly black hair. She straightened it whenever she could because that's what models looked like in magazines. Sometimes she wished she lived with her cousins in Puerto Rico, where curly hair was accepted and even thought of as pretty.

Marcus was the only boy who signed up for Future Nurses Club. Sometimes his guy friends would tease him, calling him Nurse Markie. Sometimes adults would say, "You mean you want to be a doctor, not a nurse, right?" He thought about dropping out, but he really liked the club. Marcus had a deep feeling that nursing was right for him. He loved helping sick people and didn't want the pressures of medical school. Sometimes he felt angry that people thought there was something wrong with guys being nurses.

Abby was raised in a strict religious community that had many rules about behavior. She agreed with some of the faith's values but not with others. Abby hated when people assumed she was just like the other members of her community. She was afraid to speak out about her ideas and found herself starting to break rules as a way of telling people that she was different.

Part of growing into your own identity requires exploring and discovering your own authentic ideas and ideals, your own beliefs and values. Healthy self-esteem includes having the strength and confidence to stay true to them, as long as they are safe, whether or not they go along with society's ideas.

try this

For each of the situations above, answer the following questions.

Jasmine

What social value is Jasmine affected by?

_____

How does she feel about it?

_____

What does she do about it?

_____

How do you think her self-esteem is affected by this situation?

_____

What would you do in her place?

_____

Marcus

What social value is Marcus affected by?

_____

How does he feel about it?

_____

What does he do about it?

_____

How do you think his self-esteem is affected by this situation?

_____

What would you do in his place?

_____

Abby

What social value is Abby affected by?

_____

How does she feel about it?

_____

What does she do about it?

_____

How do you think her self-esteem is affected by this situation?

_____

What would you do in her place?

_____

now try this

Circle all of the following that are sources of social pressure for you. Use the blank lines to add your own.

radio	magazines	religious leaders	_____
television	social media	teachers	_____
internet	in-person speakers	school staff	_____
billboards	politicians	gang members	_____

Over the next few days, pay attention to and record times when you are affected by your society's ideas and values. Record how your self-esteem is affected by rating it from 1 (low) to 10 (high) in the chart below or on the blank worksheet you can download at http://www.newharbinger.com/50003. For example, you might notice your self-esteem go up when you watch a TV show that praises a minority group you belong to. Or you might notice your self-esteem go down if you have freckles and see an ad for a product that gets rid of "nasty" freckles.

Day/Time	Incident	Source	Self-esteem (1–10)

Think about how your thoughts, feelings, or actions might be different if you weren't affected by your society's values.

Describe any positive changes that would occur.

_____

_____

_____

_____

_____

Describe any negative changes that would occur.

_____

_____

_____

_____

_____

today's affirmation

I can decide to let social values influence me or not.

12 it's normal to not know

know this

If you don't know exactly who your authentic self is, what you want to do with your life, or even what you want to do next year, you are perfectly normal. Most teenagers are trying to figure these things out. It is impossible to have all the answers right now.

Malia felt exhausted thinking about the career assembly earlier that morning. There had been representatives from different fields, from fast food to medicine. Malia had no idea what she wanted for her future; she had a hard enough time figuring out which classes to take.

"Sometimes I'm not even sure who I want to eat lunch with," she told her guidance counselor, Mr. Williams. "Some days I want the fun of my dance teammates and sometimes I just want to sit with Haven, who's really quiet. Some days I think I want to go to cooking school and sometimes I want to be an accountant. What's wrong with me?"

Mr. Williams assured Malia there was absolutely nothing wrong with her. "Adolescence is a time to test your ideas and explore your interests, to try out different friendships and discover the person you are most comfortable being," he said.

"But it seems like everyone else knows who they are and what they want," Malia said. "Taylor is going to be a dentist, Elizabeth wants to stay home and have six kids—and I'm not even sure if I want to join band or choir!"

"Lots of kids have ideas now," said Mr. Williams. "Some will stay on those paths, but many won't. The more we learn, the more we grow and change, and none of you have finished learning, or growing and changing. It can feel confusing and frustrating, or you might feel scared that you'll never figure it out. But it's important to remember that not knowing is completely normal. You can allow yourself to unfold one step at a time."

try this

Think back to when you were five. Try to remember anything you knew about yourself or desired for your future. Record what you remember below. Then do the same for every few years up until your current age.

Age 5 _____

Age _____ _____

Age _____ _____

Age _____ _____

Age _____ _____

Age _____ _____

Age _____ _____

How has your self-knowledge changed over time?

_____

_____

_____

How have your dreams for the future changed?

_____

_____

_____

now try this

List five to ten ideas about yourself and your future; for example, "I'm outgoing," "I'm going to cosmetology school," or "I'm going into politics." Next to each statement, write a number from 1 (not very certain) to 10 (very certain) to show how sure you feel about this idea.

_____   _____

_____   _____

_____   _____

_____   _____

Fill in the blanks below, giving yourself permission to not know everything about yourself or your future; you can also download a copy of this form at http://www .newharbinger.com/50003.

I, _____, give myself permission to _____

_____

_____

_____

_____   _____

Date   Signature

today's affirmation

It is normal to feel uncertain about exactly what I want in my future.

discovering your likes and dislikes 13

---

know this

You can learn about your authentic self by looking at what you like and don't like. No one else in the world has the exact combination of preferences and dislikes as you do.

"Today we're going to learn about ourselves by exploring our likes and dislikes," said Ms. Henning, Olivia's psychology teacher. "We make hundreds of choices every day, which are in great part determined by what we like and don't like. Every choice we make determines our behavior, moves us a little further along our path, and shapes the life we are creating for ourselves. What are some choices you make on an average day?"

"Red T-shirt or brown," said Neel.

"Bagels or cereal," said Janel.

"Watch a movie or go to the mall," said Olivia.

"Run track or play softball," said Owen.

"Our preferences come partly from experience," said Ms. Henning. "If we've done something and liked it, we want to do it again. They also come partly from biology: liking green more than yellow or hot sauce more than soy sauce. Our preferences are influenced by the way our brain and body cells react to them."

"Why are we talking about hot sauce and soy sauce?" asked Neel.

"Good question!" said Ms. Henning, smiling. "Because becoming more aware of what we like and dislike helps us strengthen our sense of self. We get a better understanding of who we are and why."

try this

Check the item in each pair below that appeals to you the most.

walk	ride	save	discard
cook	eat out	cold	hot
write	speak	numbers	words
focus	dream	day	night
books	TV	desert	mountains
home	away	give	receive
plane	car	rock	rap
hard	soft	school	work
bath	shower	air	ground
fast	slow	jeans	sweats
formal	casual	sugar	salt
meat	veggies	city	country
comedy	drama	structure	flow
cola	clear	spring	fall
alone	together	land	sea
sandals	sneakers	play	watch
curly	straight	sitcom	news
dark	light	talk	listen

Fill in the chart below to record your most and least favorite in each category:

Category	Most favorite	Least favorite	Category	Most favorite	Least favorite
movie			drink		
food			game		
song			author		
color			TV show		
class			hobby		
actor			city		
sport			video		
animal			book		
music			month		

now try this

If you could be any living creature other than a human, tell what you would like to be and why. Think about details. Would you like to fly, swim, run, or crawl? Would you rather live in the wild, a zoo, or someone's home or yard?

_____

_____

If you could be any food, tell what you would like to be and why. Would you like to be spicy? Sweet? Bitter? Would you be eaten hot or cold? Would you be a main course or a side dish?

_____

_____

Compare the description of your animal to your food. Do they seem to have similar qualities? If they are not similar, tell how they are different.

_____

_____

_____

Describe anything you think your choices tell you about yourself.

_____

_____

_____

today's affirmation

My personal likes and dislikes help me understand who I am.

discovering your dreams 14

"Today we're going to explore our dreams," said Ms. Henning. "When we daydream about the future, we usually think about the situations or people that appeal to us the most. Maybe you imagine yourself making the honor roll, going to a concert, dating someone in particular, or taking a vacation."

"I daydream about traveling somewhere with palm trees and beaches," said Janel.

"Sometimes I dream about being a vet and sometimes an engineer," said Olivia.

"I dream about living alone someday—with no brothers and sisters!" said Nathan.

"Your dreams about your future can be very clear or they might be hazy or conflicted," said Ms. Henning. "They're often affected by the way you are growing up, or how you see adults you know living their lives. You might think you want your future to be better than your parents'. You might want to carry on family traditions or make new ones."

"I dream about helping kids with disabilities, like my sister who has Down syndrome," said Ashley.

"My dream is to play pro football instead of sitting in an office like my dad," said Neel.

"When you explore your dreams for the future, you can learn more about who you are today," said Ms. Henning.

try this

To help identify some of your personal dreams, answer these questions:

If I could make three wishes come true, they would be:

1. _____
2. _____
3. _____

If I won the lottery, the first three things I would spend the money on would be:

1. _____
2. _____
3. _____

If I could travel anywhere in the world, I would go to:

1. _____
2. _____
3. _____

If I could have any talent or skill, it would be:

1. _____
2. _____
3. _____

Circle any of the following you would like to change about yourself, or add more of your own:

race	religion	ethnicity	_____
gender	country of birth	family makeup	_____
physical abilities	social abilities	intellectual abilities	_____

now try this

Find a quiet place where you won't be disturbed. Make yourself comfortable and close your eyes. Put your attention on your breath for a few minutes to help clear your mind. You don't have to change your breathing pattern; just pay attention to it. Notice where your breath moves in and out and how far it travels into your body. Let yourself relax into your breathing, feeling peace within yourself.

When you feel calm and safe, allow your mind to move into the future. Imagine that the date is five years from today. Think about what you would like your ideal day to be like five years from now. Pretend that you can make this day anything you want— there are no limits. Picture yourself waking up in the morning. Look around. What kind of setting are you in? What colors, sounds, and feelings do you experience? What is the first thing you do upon waking? What do you do next? What do you see? Whom do you interact with? Think about how you would spend your time all day if you could do anything you wanted. Whom you would be with? Where you would go?

Take as much time as you like to imagine your entire day this way, picturing everything just the way you'd like it. When you have finished this visualization, answer these questions.

Tell where you were when you woke up on your ideal day.

_____

List the things you did.

_____

_____

_____

_____

List the people you were with, if anyone.

_____

_____

_____

List the feelings you had during this day.

_____

_____

_____

What do the details you chose for your ideal day tell you about what you value and long for?

_____

_____

_____

How is your ideal day similar to what you wrote down in the "Try This" exercise?

_____

_____

_____

today's affirmation

My dreams about the future help reveal my authentic self.

know this

You can learn about your authentic self by exploring your beliefs. Your beliefs about the world, life, what is right or wrong, and what is good or bad all affect how you think, feel, and act. Some of these beliefs might reflect your authentic self; some might not.

These phrases were on the board when Olivia walked into psychology class:

How the world was created

What the drinking age should be

Whether the dress code in our school is fair

How much power the government should have

Whether there is life after death

"We all have beliefs about these topics," said Ms. Henning. "Our belief systems may be influenced by our families, our friends, our ethnic and religious traditions, and everything we learn as we grow up. Beliefs exist across all categories. They may be strong or mild, rational or irrational. They may be certain or open to change. Who can share some beliefs you learned as a child?"

"My family has a strong belief about education," said Brayden. "Ever since we were born, my parents have told my brothers and me that we will go to college."

"My parents say, 'Honesty is the best policy,'" said Janel.

"My dad says, 'The government should get off our backs,'" said Neel.

"My aunt and my mom are always telling me what they say in church," said Olivia. "It's better to give than to receive."

"Those are all good examples," said Ms. Henning. "Sometimes we carry on the beliefs we're taught because we agree with them. Sometimes we continue believing them just because we never stopped to question whether they're right for us.

"Whatever your beliefs are, you have a right to them. They help you make choices about the life you're creating for yourself. When you explore your belief systems, you can understand yourself better."

try this

Make a list of the ideas or beliefs you grew up hearing repeatedly, whether from your family, friends, or society. To the left of each, circle the up arrow if you agree with this belief and the down arrow if you disagree with it.

↑ ↓ 1. _____

↑ ↓ 2. _____

↑ ↓ 3. _____

↑ ↓ 4. _____

↑ ↓ 5. _____

Rewrite any beliefs you disagree with, changing them to more accurately reflect your personal beliefs.

1. _____

2. _____

3. _____

4. _____

5. _____

Circle the number that most closely represents what percentage of time you act on beliefs that don't reflect your authentic self.

10%   20%   30%   40%   50%   60%   70%   80%   90%   100%

now try this

Choose five or more of the following questions to answer from your personal beliefs, not just what others have told you. Your beliefs may be the same or different from your friends' or family's. You might not be sure about your beliefs on any of these topics, and that's okay.

Which environmental issues are the most important?

_____

Which political stance makes the most sense to you: liberal, moderate, or conservative?

_____

What do you believe about war?

_____

Should it be easier or harder to get divorced?

_____

Should your state's drinking age be changed? _____

Should your state's driving age be changed? _____

Would wearing school uniforms help students feel more equal to each other?

_____

Under what circumstances is it okay to have sex?

_____

Is spanking children okay?

_____

Is there a God? _____

What happens to people after they die?

_____

How was human life created?

_____

Should abortion be legal? _____

Should all people have the right to own a gun?

_____

Should the death penalty be abolished?

_____

What kinds of rights or services should illegal immigrants have?

_____

Should street drugs be legalized?

_____

Should legal marriage be available for all genders?

_____

today's affirmation

My beliefs help me understand what is important to me.

discovering your passions 16

On the final day of class, Olivia's teacher announced they would be talking about passion. Some of the students laughed. "I thought we only talked about that in health class!" someone said.

"You're thinking of sexual passion," said Ms. Henning. "That's an example of passion, but only one kind. A passion can be anything that moves you deeply, from an idea to a hobby to a person. We usually feel a strong commitment to our passions, a connection that goes beyond a thinking level. We can feel our passions physically, emotionally, and spiritually; they run stronger and deeper than likes and dislikes. Who can name a passion they have and tell how it affects them?"

"Animal rights," said Owen. "I've seen movies and read articles about how cruelly animals are treated on factory farms. Lots of them are confined to small cages and can't even stand up their whole lives. That's why I'm a vegetarian."

"Don't laugh," said Nathan, "but my passion is my baseball collection! I've got autographed baseballs from nine major leaguers, and I'm hoping to get number ten this summer. Once I found my brother playing with one, and I got really mad. They're pretty important to me."

"Dance," said Ashley. "I've taken lessons since kindergarten, and I don't know if I'll ever stop. I love how I feel when I'm dancing."

"I guess I feel passionate about my boyfriend," said Olivia. "Not only in a physical way, but I just like being with him so much. We both like skiing and horror movies and pizza with everything on it. He's kind and honest, and he makes me laugh. I guess he's my best friend."

"Good," said Ms. Henning. "You've identified that we can feel passionate about ideas, possessions, activities, and people. Identifying your passions can increase your awareness of your authentic self."

try this

Circle any of the following ideas, possessions, activities, people, or animals you feel passionate about.

Ideas

politics	civil rights	religion	the arts	education
animal rights	divorce	freedom	peace	health

Possessions

jewelry	clothes	books	sports equipment	cars
money	computers	phones	works of art	music

Activities

learning	socializing	athletics	art	music	travel
volunteering	eating	sleeping	being outdoors		reading

People/Animals

endangered animals	my friends	my family	the human race	the sick
the homeless	my pets	people with disabilities	my siblings	my boy- or girlfriend

In this frame, describe your passions more personally through writing or drawing. For example, you might write someone's name or how you feel about mandatory school attendance or draw your favorite hobby.

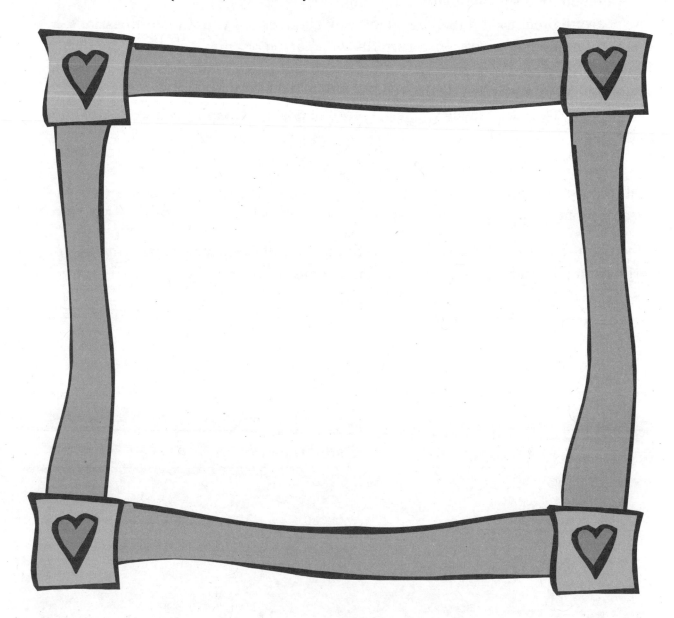

now try this

Take a few minutes to sit quietly and comfortably, close your eyes, and relax. Take a few peaceful breaths, and then begin to think about one of your greatest passions. It might be an idea, a possession, an activity, or a person or animal. Create a detailed visualization of yourself involved with this passion. As you watch yourself, notice how your body responds. What feelings arise? Where do you feel them? Maybe you notice a tingling or warmth. Maybe you feel a sense of positive energy in part or all of your body.

Continue to imagine yourself involved with your passion and enjoy the feelings that this picture evokes. When you are ready, gently bring your attention back to the present moment and open your eyes.

When you've finished and while your feelings are still fresh, take a few minutes to write from your heart about what this passion means to you.

_____

_____

_____

_____

_____

today's affirmation

My passions help tell me who I am.

---

know this

When you are struggling to decide how to handle a life challenge, try looking at it from a bigger perspective. Look beyond the personalities and the problem and ask yourself, *Who do I want to be in the universe?* to help make behavior choices that are in line with your authentic self.

When facing a challenging situation you're not sure how to handle, it's easy to get caught up in confusion, frustration, or pain. You may think through option after option, trying to predict what would happen if you acted one way or another. You may try to second-guess what people will think or say in response to your choice. You may spend a lot of time worrying that you'll end up feeling embarrassed or upset.

We get caught up in insecure thinking by letting other people's potential reactions drive our decisions. If we always let what other people think sway us, we'll never have peace of mind. We'll just shift from one side of the fence to the other and back again, trying to do what we think others want us to.

We can get out of this mess by looking at the situation from a bigger perspective. Instead of asking, *What will they think of me?* we ask, *Who do I want to be in the universe?*

This question draws our minds to the bigger ideas of who we really are and what we want to contribute to this planet. What kind of person do we want to be? What kind of values do we want to live by? How do we want to relate to others?

Asking this question can help us think more clearly about behavior choices that will keep us true to our authentic selves.

try this

Make a list of people you admire for the way they live their lives. These might be family members, friends, public figures, or people from history. Next to each name, write what quality of that person's character you would like to develop in yourself.

_____

_____

_____

_____

_____

Answer the following:

What do I want to stand for?

_____

_____

_____

What do I want to contribute to the planet?

_____

_____

_____

_____

What would I like to be remembered for?

_____

_____

_____

If you had the power to change the world, tell what it would look like when you were done.

_____

_____

_____

_____

_____

_____

_____

_____

now try this

Think about the kind of person you want to be, and tell how you would act in each of the following situations.

You are with friends at the mall and see a girl ahead of you walking with a limp. One of your friends starts to walk with a pretend limp, and soon the rest are laughing and doing the same. They want you to join in. The girl looks back, and you see the pain and embarrassment on her face.

_____

_____

_____

A good friend borrows your favorite shirt and gets a huge stain on the front. It won't wash out, and the shirt is ruined.

_____

_____

_____

Your little brother annoys you all the time. You see some bigger kids at the bus stop hassling him and grabbing his backpack.

_____

_____

_____

Your cousin wants you to do his homework for him because he doesn't understand it. He says it's not really cheating because you go to different schools.

_____

_____

_____

After an argument with your best friend, he refuses to talk to you. All your other friends say you are in the right.

_____

_____

_____

Now think of a real-life conflict you are having with someone or another situation that's troubling you. Tell how you could act based on your ideals.

_____

_____

_____

_____

_____

today's affirmation

I choose my actions by thinking about who I want to be in the universe.

18 why you are here

know this

Because you are the only person with your specific combination of talents, skills, and gifts, you have a unique contribution to make to the universe. Understanding this concept, exploring it, and staying true to your path will help you live your truth no matter what others may say or do.

When you start listening to the authentic voice within you, you will get a clearer idea about what is best for you and what isn't, including which paths in life are right for you.

These may be daily paths you encounter when deciding whether to play basketball or volleyball, babysit or take a fast-food job, or become friends with one group or another. Or they may be bigger paths that stretch out further into the future, leading to career and life choices. There is no one else exactly like you, so there is no one else whose path is exactly right for you.

No one can fill the very same purpose as another human being. Learning about your unique purpose can give you greater confidence in your value and the special contribution you alone can make to the world. Understanding that purpose, or coming closer to it, can give you something to believe in when you feel uncertain or vulnerable. Knowing without doubt that you are alive for a special reason can give you the strength to remain true to your convictions when others try to persuade you to move away from them.

Important Note: If what you believe to be your purpose might lead you to act in an illegal, immoral, or unethical way, or to do something that will get you into trouble, *check it out*. It is most likely a misguided thought. A true, healthy purpose will rarely lead to a negative consequence.

try this

Great artists, inventors, and people of wisdom have always followed their given purpose to find success. Write the names of real people you know who you think are living their true life purpose, and tell why you think they are.

_____

_____

_____

_____

_____

If you have the chance, talk to these people about their experiences. You might ask them when they first knew their purpose, how it may have changed over time, or what steps they took to pursue it. Record their answers here.

_____

_____

_____

_____

_____

_____

_____

now try this

You may have a good idea of what your life purpose is, or you may have no idea at all. Either way, it's okay. If you keep exploring and accepting your authentic self, you will eventually find your purpose.

Rate each activity listed below on a scale of 1 (low) to 10 (high) according to how appealing it sounds to you. Try to respond from your intuition rather than thinking too much. Add any more of your own.

____ swimming with dolphins   ____ planning a city

____ caring for people   ____ speaking passionately

____ teaching children   ____ inspiring people

____ being outdoors   ____ working at a computer

____ using your mind   ____ moving your body

____ sailing a boat   ____ playing with children

____ working with technology   ____ working with numbers

____ leading others   ____ writing books

____ traveling internationally   ____ having your own business

____ serving others   ____ playing sports

____ maintaining a household   ____ working with animals

____ improving health conditions   ____ improving the environment

____ _____   ____ _____

____ _____   ____ _____

Which activities did you rate higher than 5?

_____

_____

Which did you rate 5 or lower?

_____

_____

Describe any patterns you see in your ratings.

_____

_____

_____

Make a list of your natural talents and gifts.

_____

_____

_____

_____

How do your ratings compare to your talents and gifts?

_____

_____

_____

When you find yourself struggling with self-doubt or caught up in negative details, ask yourself:

Who am I here to help?

_____

What am I here to do?

_____

What is my purpose today?

_____

Ask one or two people who know you well to tell you what they think your purpose might be. Have them tell you their reasoning. Record their answers below and then write your own thoughts about whether you agree or disagree with them and why.

_____

_____

_____

_____

_____

_____

today's affirmation

Remembering that I have a unique purpose in life helps
me stay true to myself.

celebrate your strengths, work with your weaknesses 19

know this

Everyone on the planet has both strengths and weaknesses. Having healthy self-esteem means that you both recognize and celebrate your strengths and you accept and work with your weaknesses. You understand that neither one affects your innate value and worth as a human being.

If you're alive, you have strengths. There's no person without them. Your strengths might be physical, like being good at field hockey, tai chi, cooking, or horseback riding; or they might be intellectual, like excelling at chemistry, computer science, or problem solving. They might be emotional, like staying calm in a crisis, showing compassion, or having patience. Maybe your strengths are being generous, organized, loyal, hardworking, or reliable, or expressing yourself clearly. When you recognize and celebrate the things you're good at and the qualities you're proud of, you build healthy self-esteem.

No one likes having weaknesses, but they don't have to damage your self-esteem. Perfection doesn't exist on this planet, so if you get down on yourself for not being good at everything or friends with everyone or smart in every subject, you're fighting a losing battle. A healthier habit is to accept your weaknesses and then, if necessary, work on improving them. Some weaknesses don't matter much, like if you're not good at trigonometry and you want to be a massage therapist. But if you have social anxiety and want to run for public office, you'll probably need to conquer that. If you can't crack an egg without it shooting all over the floor and you want to be a pastry chef, you'll need to improve. But if you want to be an accountant and don't like eggs anyway, it doesn't matter.

try this

Strengths can include areas where you've won or achieved something; they can also include what you attempt, what you think, and who you are. Just reading this book reflects strength. It means you're willing to try something new. It means you have hope and courage and are open to change.

Circle any of the following strengths that are true about you. Then add at least five more of your own on the lines that follow.

good listener	loving	good musician
kind to animals	responsible	good party planner
good sense of humor	honest	good writer
patient	reliable	healthy eater
sincere	smart	flexible
clean	good friend	_____
loyal	brave	_____
talented at a sport	talented at a hobby	_____
hardworking	persevering	_____
kind to people	good researcher	_____

Ask three or more people what they would name as your strengths and record their answers here.

1. _____

2. _____

3. _____

now try this

Identify up to five areas where you could use improvement. Maybe you have a hard time telling the truth, being on time, taking tests, winning at a particular game, or making friends.

1. _____

2. _____

3. _____

4. _____

5. _____

Rate each area on a scale of 1 (low) to 10 (high) according to how important improving this is in order to achieve your life goals.

Next list the areas you want to work on in order of importance. After each, write a short-term and a long-term goal that you can work toward to improve. Finally, write realistic dates for starting and accomplishing each goal.

Area to work on _____

Short-term goal _____

Starting date _____   Date for accomplishing _____

Long-term goal _____

Starting date _____   Date for accomplishing _____

Area to work on _____

Short-term goal _____

Starting date _____   Date for accomplishing _____

Long-term goal _____

Starting date _____   Date for accomplishing _____

Area to work on _____

Short-term goal _____

Starting date _____   Date for accomplishing _____

Long-term goal _____

Starting date _____   Date for accomplishing _____

Area to work on _____

Short-term goal _____

Starting date _____   Date for accomplishing _____

Long-term goal _____

Starting date _____   Date for accomplishing _____

Area to work on _____

Short-term goal _____

Starting date _____   Date for accomplishing _____

Long-term goal _____

Starting date _____   Date for accomplishing _____

today's affirmation

I honor and celebrate my strengths and accept and work with my
weaknesses to maintain healthy self—esteem.

know this

Discovering and listening to your intuition or "inner voice" can lead you to your authentic self and the path that is right for you. When you learn to trust your authentic self, you can better know and follow your true path.

Sometimes we have a strong, deep feeling about what is right for us. Maybe we've always wanted to teach, practice medicine, or climb mountains. Maybe we are drawn to a particular sport or hobby. When we think about it, we may not know exactly why we want to do this; we just know it is a deep yearning, and when we participate in this activity it feels good.

Sometimes we have a strong, deep feeling about making a decision—we just know that one decision is right and another is not. We may also have a strong, deep feeling that something is going to happen. We might think, *I have a feeling Mariah will call soon,* or *I have a feeling I'll be back here.*

This strong, deep feeling is called intuition. The messages from intuition are both felt in our bodies and heard in our minds. Sometimes these messages are not in agreement with logic. Sometimes we don't listen to them and then we think, *I knew I shouldn't have done that—why didn't I listen to my intuition?*

Paying attention to our intuitive messages can help us find our authentic selves. Staying true to those selves can help us build and maintain healthy self-esteem.

try this

Without thinking—just using your "gut feeling" or intuition—circle the answers that are right for you.

Which color appeals to you most?

red   orange   yellow   blue   green   purple   brown   black   white

Which shape or line appeals to you most?

Which number appeals to you most?

6   3   10   2   5   8   4   9   7   1

Which symbol appeals to you most?

Which font appeals to you most?

this one   this one   *this one*   THIS ONE   THIS ONE

Name any people you feel you just click with or connect with in an unexplainable way.

_____

_____

_____

_____

_____

Some people experience a deep knowing that they want to be an architect or a parent or to travel or study art. Describe any deep knowings you have about your future.

_____

_____

_____

Describe any time you may have "felt" an answer in your body. Maybe it was a tightening in your chest or a quickening of your heartbeat.

_____

_____

_____

Describe any time you felt yourself drawn to something or someone, as if there were a magnetic pull between you.

_____

_____

_____

Describe any other time in your life when you noticed your intuition speaking to you.

_____

_____

_____

now try this

For the next few days, pay attention to and record any hunches you have. Hunches don't always follow logic. They are thoughts or feelings that you sense rather than know intellectually; for example, *I have a feeling it's going to rain*, or *I have a feeling we'll win although the odds are with the other team.*

Important Note: If your intuition ever tells you to do something that is illegal, immoral, or unethical, or will get you into trouble, *check it out*. It is most likely a misguided thought, as real intuition will rarely lead to a negative consequence.

Day 1 hunches: _____

_____

_____

Day 2 hunches: _____

_____

_____

Day 3 hunches: _____

_____

_____

To practice moving past your intellect and listening internally, try these exercises. When you are done, describe what each activity was like for you.

- Sit quietly and comfortably with several sheets of blank paper or your computer or mobile device. Clear your mind, and write, "I remember…" Follow with any thoughts that come. Continue writing anything that arises, without thinking about it or judging. Ignore spelling, grammar, punctuation, and any other writing rules you've learned. Simply let your intuitive mind take over and express whatever comes up. Write for as long as you feel comfortable.

_____

_____

_____

- Sit quietly and comfortably, and close your eyes. Take a few relaxing breaths, and watch as a scene unfolds in your mind. Let your imagination lead you wherever it will. What do you notice about what appears to you?

_____

_____

_____

- At any time during the day, stop your activity for a moment and tune in to yourself. Feel your heartbeat and your breath. Notice what your muscles are doing and let them relax. Close your eyes and feel the energy that animates you. When you have turned yourself inward, simply listen. Pay attention to any inner messages you get.

_____

_____

_____

- Pay attention to how you respond to people and situations. When you find yourself clinging to rigid thinking, try to let go and open your mind. Let answers and actions come to you from your intuition rather than always filling them in from your brain. Notice how this affects you.

_____

_____

_____

- When it is safe and healthy to do so, make choices that bring you joy. The feeling of joy is deeper and more all-encompassing than happiness. Feeling true joy is usually a signal that we are following our intuition and being true to our authentic selves.

_____

_____

_____

today's affirmation

My intuition is a message from my authentic self.

your body image: how to fight false facts 21

---

know this

Self-esteem is often affected by how we think our looks compare to the cultural beauty ideal. When that beauty ideal is impossible to meet yet is promoted by a business to sell products, sales go up while self-esteem goes down. The repeated pattern of buying but then failing to meet the ideal helps the business thrive but causes buyers to feel bad about themselves. No matter how many diet, exercise, toning, covering, and looks-changing products they buy, they still can't meet the impossible ideal.

Savannah came home from the gymnastics meet feeling great. She'd received her highest score on the trampoline, and she'd also aced her chemistry test that morning. She wanted to relax a little before doing homework, so she started scrolling through internet fashion ads to see what was new. But after only a few minutes, Savannah felt her happiness dissolving. She was looking at swimsuit ads. The models were all far thinner and taller than she was; they all had perfect skin and they all had perfect-looking partners at their sides. Who cares what I do on the tramp or in school? *Savannah thought.* I'll never look like that.

The next day in assembly, a guest speaker described how photos of models, both electronic and print, are digitally altered before publication. She demonstrated how with one touch of the keyboard, she could make eyes wider, skin clearer, thighs thinner, and muscles more toned. "It's important to know that what we see in ads is not reality; the images have been photoshopped, retouched, or airbrushed," she said.

The speaker also talked about the big business of selling a beauty ideal. "Billions of dollars are spent each year to keep us believing there's only one 'right' way to look. These are arbitrary opinions that change through the decades. In ancient Greece it was important for the distance between nipples and navel to be equal. In legendary actress Marilyn Monroe's time, voluptuous curves were valued. Some years males 'should' be lean, other times bulging with muscle.

"When we buy into an unrealistic arbitrary beauty ideal, we also buy beauty and diet products, and the industry makes a lot of money. When the models aren't even 'real,' we can never match them, so we never stop buying. But we have a choice. We don't have to be controlled by a business. We can learn to take back our power and think for ourselves."

Savannah thought about all of this and felt angry but empowered. She decided to stop judging her looks so harshly and letting her self-esteem be determined by people who didn't even know her.

try this

Over the next few days, pay attention to the cultural messages you hear about the "right" way to look. Circle their sources.

television	internet	other
print ads	movies	_____
radio	mall advertising	_____
billboards	social media	_____

Record the messages you heard here. Then circle the T next to those that are true, or circle the dollar sign next to those created to make money.

T $ _____

T $ _____

T $ _____

T $ _____

T $ _____

T $ _____

T $ _____

T $ _____

Tell how each of these messages affect your self-esteem.

_____

_____

_____

now try this

Write your intention to take back control of your feelings about your looks from a big business.

_____

_____

Use the sources above or find others that promote a beauty ideal that's unachievable by the average person. Print or copy these ads or messages and then shred or (safely) destroy them in some other way. List the messages you destroyed and then describe what it was like to do this.

_____

_____

_____

_____

_____

How does it affect your self-esteem when you take charge of your feelings about your looks in this way?

_____

_____

_____

If you ran the universe and could change the idea of "the right way to look," what would you do about this?

_____

_____

_____

_____

_____

_____

_____

today's affirmation

I refuse to compare myself to an ideal that doesn't actually exist or let a business tell me how I should look just so it can make money.

22 your body image: how to love the body you've got

know this

Focusing on what we don't like about our bodies makes us feel bad about ourselves. Focusing on all that is amazing and positive about our bodies helps create healthy self-esteem.

Brianna was bigger than any girl and most boys in her class. She was tall and large-boned and felt like a giant. She tried to slouch and eat less to become smaller but nothing worked, and every day she hated the way she looked. One day the swim coach approached her. "Why don't you celebrate your body instead of berating it?" Ms. Clark asked. "Long, strong arms and legs can really move through water." Brianna joined the swim team and began breaking records. She stopped worrying about how her body compared to others and became grateful for it instead.

We come into the world loving our bodies, fascinated by how our legs kick and fingers wiggle. But as we grow we start hearing messages that say bodies are valuable only if they look a certain way. We forget the true purposes of our bodies: to see, hear, swallow, think, touch, digest, rest, heal, taste, take in fuel, move from place to place, and recreate ourselves. We forget about these miracles when we focus on looks. We also damage our self-esteem when we buy into the false belief that our value is connected to how we look and that we'd be happy if only we were taller, shorter, thinner, more or less muscular, clear-skinned, fair-skinned, or darker skinned.

Having healthy self-esteem means you recognize that all bodies are different and are supposed to be that way. You stop thinking negatively about this awesome machine and start loving your body for the miracle it is. You appreciate the "mobile home" that carries you wherever you want to go, lets you water-ski, sleep, taste pizza, rock climb, hug, kiss, laugh, curl up on the couch, and see a sunset. When you shift from criticizing your body to appreciating all that's right with it, your self-esteem can grow.

try this

These words and phrases describe parts of your physical body. Next to each, write its purpose. Put a star next to those for which you are grateful.

_____ veins	_____ heart	_____ toenails
_____ elbows	_____ eardrums	_____ nipples
_____ leg bones	_____ teeth	_____ navel
_____ lungs	_____ kneecaps	_____ digestive system
_____ eyeballs	_____ skin	_____ taste buds
_____ fingers	_____ nostrils	_____ reproductive organs

Make a list of twenty or more ways your body has helped you since you were born, no matter what it looked like. This could be anything from being able to see colors, wake up in the morning, heal a cut, recover from a cold, or win a Frisbee tournament.

Write a thoughtful and loving letter to one or more parts of your body. Let each part know how thankful you are for what it has done and continues to do for you.

now try this

These people will be studied and remembered for generations to come. Circle those whose contribution to society had anything to do with the way they looked.

Martin Luther King Jr.	Florence Nightingale	Marie Curie
Abraham Lincoln	Mahatma Gandhi	J.K. Rowling
William Shakespeare	Amelia Earhart	Thomas Edison
Albert Einstein	Nelson Mandela	Maya Angelou
Mother Teresa	Eleanor Roosevelt	Galileo

Write the names of the three most important people in your life. Tell what makes each of them valuable to you.

_____

_____

_____

_____

_____

_____

Then ask one of these people what makes you valuable to them and record it here.

_____

_____

_____

How many times was "looks" reported as a valuable quality? How many qualities other than "looks" were named?

_____

_____

Describe what you as an individual, with your own unique talents and strengths, would like to contribute to the planet during your lifetime. (A positive change for society? Love or caring for others? Discovering a cure for disease? Helping people who are less fortunate? Good looks?)

_____

_____

_____

_____

_____

_____

_____

_____

today's affirmation

I love my body for all the amazing ways it helps me enjoy my life.

know this

Human beings often judge each other because it helps them temporarily feel better about themselves. People who put you down might think they are better than you. If you put others down, you might think you are better than them. But it's not true. Self-worth exists as a truth, independent of any outside judgments. When we have healthy self-esteem, we recognize that and don't need to judge others or let their judgments bother us.

Anika and some friends were standing by her locker. When Avery walked by, two of the girls rolled their eyes. "Can you believe her?" one asked. "How could she wear something like that to school?"

"She's crazy," said another. "What do you expect?"

In science class, Anika overheard some kids making rude comments about a particular minority. They were making fun of them, making generalizations, and being critical of people they didn't know.

That night at a party, Anika's good friend Isaac called her selfish when Anika said she wouldn't lie to his date for him. Anika felt really upset and left. When she got home, her mother could tell something was wrong and asked what had happened.

"I'm tired of people judging each other so negatively," said Anika. "Why do we do that? We say such mean and unfair things about other people all the time." She told her mom about the three situations.

"People usually make judgments to feel better about themselves," said Anika's mom. "When we criticize someone else's looks or lifestyle, somewhere deep inside we think, I'm not as bad as that. Or sometimes we are feeling negative and unfairly let it out on another person.

"Your girlfriends and the kids in class may feel superior when they talk that way about others. Isaac may have felt frustrated about the problems with his date, or guilty because he knew he shouldn't ask you to lie for him. He was covering up his real feelings by criticizing you. That's why it's important not to take those judgments personally. Judging says more about the person doing the judging than about the one being judged."

try this

Judging others doesn't make us any better than them; it doesn't make us right and them wrong; it doesn't make us more valuable and them less valuable. All judging does is make us feel temporarily (and falsely) better about ourselves.

For one day, pay attention to the judgmental statements you hear from people in the following categories. Try to find and record at least two in each category.

Family

_____

_____

Friends

_____

_____

Acquaintances

_____

_____

Strangers

_____

_____

Myself

_____

_____

Do any of these judgments actually make the criticisms true? _____

Explain why the following speakers may have made these judgments:

"She's stuck up because she's in all honors classes. She's probably boring because all she does is study."

_____

_____

_____

"The people who live over there are awful. I'm glad I'm not one of them."

_____

_____

_____

"He's really handsome, but girls probably just use him because they want to be seen with a cute guy."

_____

_____

_____

"Do you always have to be in such a good mood? It's so irritating."

_____

_____

_____

now try this

Try going through one day without judging others. When you notice judgmental thoughts, try to replace them with accepting thoughts. Describe two specific examples of situations in which you changed your thoughts.

1. _____

_____

_____

2. _____

_____

_____

Tell what it was like to let go of judgment.

_____

_____

_____

_____

Describe a recent situation in which you heard a negative judgment about yourself.

_____

_____

_____

_____

_____

What did you tell yourself? What feelings did your thoughts create? How did this affect your self-esteem?

_____

_____

_____

_____

_____

_____

_____

_____

today's affirmation

Another person's judgment does not change my self-worth.

24 take charge of social media

know this

Using social media has many benefits such as staying connected, sharing life experiences, educational and business opportunities, and developing technical skills. But when not used in a healthy way, social media can also damage our self-esteem. It's important to recognize how social media affects you, and to make smart choices about how and when you connect.

If you're not paying attention, it's easy to get caught up in a self-defeating social media web. Being aware of the following social media pitfalls can help you steer clear of the aspects that can undermine self-esteem.

Unrealistic comparing. Posts on social media can damage self-esteem because we view only the best parts of other peoples' lives and then we compare those images and updates to the worst parts of our own lives. This causes feelings of failure, inadequacy, dissatisfaction with ourselves, and anxiety, all of which lower self-esteem. It also motivates us to set unrealistic goals because we want to "be like them," and when we can't meet those goals we feel worse.

Cyberbullying. Cyberbullying is a way of using social media to hurt or harass another person in any way. Examples include sending online threats, mean or rude texts, tweets, posts, or messages; spreading rumors or lies; posting or refusing to take down photos, personal information, or videos to purposely threaten, embarrass, or upset someone. Cyberbullying is often repeated over and over, making the recipient feel angry, sad, scared, and bad about themself.

Fear of missing out (FOMO). FOMO is an anxious condition that damages healthy self-esteem. It stems from the thought that we're missing out on something—either someone else's seemingly "better" life, or a party or social event, or even just getting information. FOMO increases the feeling that other people are having more fun than we are or have far more awesome lives than ours.

try this

Think about your own social media use in relation to the problems listed above. How does social media affect your self-esteem? Give an example.

_____

_____

_____

Have you ever been a victim of cyberbullying? What was this like for you?

_____

_____

_____

_____

Have you ever bullied someone else online? What motivated you to do this?

_____

_____

_____

_____

Do you ever experience FOMO and find yourself checking your phone or device compulsively? How does this affect your self-esteem?

_____

_____

_____

Over the next few days, keep track of your self-esteem both before and after spending time on social media. Use a 1 (low self-esteem) to 10 (healthy self-esteem) rating scale. Record your observations in the chart below. If you need more space, you can download this chart at http://www.newharbinger.com/50003.

Day	Time	Number of minutes spent	Social media platform	Self-esteem at start	Self-esteem at end

What can you learn about yourself from the information in your chart?

_____

_____

_____

now try this

The following tips can both help the way you process social media and help you cut back on your usage. Try any or all of these to prevent damaging your self-esteem.

Reframe your perspective about social media posts. It's important to remember that the photos and updates you see tell only one part of someone's story: the part they want to publicize. Everyone who posts something cool also has tons of uncool info they don't want others to know. Also, remember that people use photo-altering tools— so you're probably comparing yourself to something that isn't even real. Social media doesn't show real life but a perfected version, and there's *no one* who can live up to that.

Cut off cyberbullying. If you receive a negative message, stop it right there by not responding or retaliating. Block the sender and then report the comments to the appropriate platform. Don't reread the comments. Recognize that happy, secure people don't need to bully others; rude comments are more about the issues of the sender than you, so they shouldn't be taken personally. Keep your social media settings high to keep your privacy more secure. Talk to someone you trust about your experience; sharing your feelings will help you recover.

Try JOMO instead of FOMO. JOMO is the joy of missing out. It means being in the present moment, enjoying what you're doing instead of worrying about what others are doing. It means living your own life to the fullest, finding what brings you joy, and delighting in that experience of life and of yourself right now. It means embracing the gift of your own life instead of trying to live someone else's.

Turn your phone to grayscale and limit your home screen apps. Tech experts tell us our phone screens are purposely designed with bright colors to draw us in like bait and fixate our brains, making it hard to look away or put down. Turning off unnecessary push notifications and distracting apps and changing your display to black and white short-circuits this tendency by making the visual less exciting. Put yourself back in charge of what you bring in to your device and your mind.

Help your brain stop scrolling. The brain pathways stimulated by constant scrolling on a device are the same ones stimulated in a chemical addiction. Help your brain shift gears by giving it something else to do. If you're triggered to stay online because you're feeling overwhelmed, bored, tired or lonely, make a conscious effort to find real-life solutions or distractions through nonmedia sources like friends, family, nature, music, art, exercise, or sports.

Try a social media detox. Set aside one day, one part of a day, or at least a block of a few hours each week where you stay off social media and stop judging yourself. Go outside, work out, meet a friend in person, play a silly game with your younger sib, paint, dance, bake, surf a real ocean wave instead of the internet. Use your body and brain to interact, balance your digital life with real life, clear your head and get regrounded in healthy self-esteem.

Which of these tips helped your self-esteem the most?

_____

Which was the hardest to implement?

_____

Which do you think would be most beneficial for you to keep working on?

_____

On a scale from 1 (low) to 10 (high), tell how hard it is for you to reframe your thoughts about social media.

_____

Using the same scale, how hard is it for you to cut back on social media use?

_____

Tell what you could do to help yourself realistically work on maintaining healthy self-esteem while still using social media.

_____

_____

_____

_____

_____

_____

_____

today's affirmation

I use social media wisely and keep it in perspective
to maintain healthy self-esteem.

25 how to talk to people: basic social skills

know this

You don't have to be a brilliant conversationalist to be comfortable talking to or being with other people. Just using basic social skills can start to raise your confidence in communicating and interacting. When you realize you can do this, you create healthier self-esteem.

Sometimes we think we need a special quality or an amazing personality to feel comfortable talking to people. We might think people who make friends easily have some magical trait that draws others to them. These thoughts create anxiety in social situations, especially with new people. We tell ourselves we'll have nothing to say or whatever we say will sound dumb. We forget our intrinsic value and equality to everyone else. We forget that other people have weaknesses and challenges, too, even if we can't see them.

You probably know or use some basic social skills already and just don't realize it. For example, if you're at your first student council meeting, you might smile, say hello to people, and listen to others without interrupting. If you're asking someone if you can borrow some paper, you say "Please" and "Thank you." If you accidentally bump into someone in the hallway, you say "Excuse me." You treat others the way you would like to be treated yourself.

Talking to other people is a skill that can be learned, and like everything else, the more you practice the better you get. Getting in the habit of using the following six basic social skills can increase your confidence and build healthy self-esteem.

- **Use good manners.** Good manners mean speaking and acting in ways that are polite, friendly, and respectful of others such as saying "please," "thank you," and "excuse me," and not interrupting when someone else is talking.

- **Remember "AL."** *Ask* and *listen* more than you talk. People quickly tire of those who only talk on and on about themselves. Asking about the other person and listening carefully to their answers is one of the best gifts you can give someone.

- **Use the Five Ws for conversation starters.** If you can't think of anything to say, start with *who, what, when, where,* or *why*. (Who do you have for math this year? What are you doing over vacation? When does the new movie come out? Where did you get your backpack? Why did he give so much homework today?)

- **Smile and be positive.** Positivity makes us feel good. When you smile, and talk and act positively, people enjoy being with you more.

- **Give and accept compliments.** Look for something you like and let the person know: "I like your sandals," "You're so thoughtful." When you receive a compliment, smile and say thanks. Rejecting a compliment is like refusing a gift.

- **Remember the Golden Rule.** How would you like others to treat you? With courtesy, respect, compassion, acceptance, kindness? Practice those same qualities with others. That's what they want too.

try this

Describe how you usually feel when you have to make conversation with other people and tell why.

_____

_____

_____

_____

_____

Tell how your ability to talk to other people affects your self-esteem.

_____

_____

_____

_____

Practice thinking of questions you could ask or comments you could make to the following people using the above six guidelines. Write two or more conversation starters you could use for each situation.

Someone who's standing at your school bus stop

_____

_____

_____

_____

Someone who's been assigned to do a history project with you

_____

_____

_____

_____

Someone whose locker is next to yours

_____

_____

_____

_____

Someone standing next to you in the cafeteria line

_____

_____

_____

_____

Someone sitting next to you in the bleachers at a basketball game

_____

_____

_____

_____

now try this

Describe a situation you were in recently when you could have used any of the social skills listed above, and tell which would have been most helpful.

_____

_____

_____

_____

_____

Tell which of these skills is the easiest for you to use and why.

_____

_____

_____

_____

Tell which of these skills is the hardest for you to use and why.

_____

_____

_____

_____

Over the next couple of days practice using the six basic social skills. Use the chart below or download a blank worksheet at http://www.newharbinger.com/50003, and write the name of the person you talked to, the skills you used, and how well things went.

Name	Skill	How it went

today's affirmation

I use basic social skills to help me start talking to people with confidence.

26 assertive communication

know this

Assertiveness is a style of communication based in respect for oneself and respect for others. When you use assertive communication, you build healthy self-esteem because you have more legitimate successes both in relationships and with achieving goals.

There are three main communication styles: passive, aggressive, and assertive. If someone cuts in front of you in line and you feel very angry and think really mean thoughts about them in your head but say nothing, you're acting passively. If you shove that person and push them to the ground, you're acting aggressively. If you calmly say, "Excuse me, I was already here," you're acting assertively.

Assertiveness is the most positive form of communication because its goal is to respect both your rights and the rights of others. When you act assertively, you feel good about yourself because you're cooperating with other people at the same time you're standing up for yourself, and you're doing it in a healthy way. You also get more positive outcomes that build heathy self-esteem. For example:

Jayden thought his essay had been graded unfairly. He reacted passively by slumping in his chair and thinking negative thoughts about himself, his teacher, and the class. This made him feel disappointed, angry, and sad. His grade remained the same.

Addison thought her essay had been graded unfairly. She reacted aggressively by slamming her fist into her desk, swearing loudly, and storming out of the classroom. She got sent to the dean and was grounded by her parents. She yelled about how badly everyone treated her and felt angry, bitter and resentful. Her grade remained the same.

Ash thought their essay had been graded unfairly. They reacted assertively by making an appointment with the teacher, who listened to Ash's reasoning and then explained her own side. Both the teacher and Ash felt good about the other person because they'd each been heard and respected. The teacher agreed with some of Ash's reasoning and raised their grade by five points.

try this

Read these situations and the statements below them. Write "passive," "assertive," or "aggressive" for each statement, according to the behavior it illustrates.

You pay for a two-scoop ice cream cone but only get one scoop.

You yell, "This place is a rip-off!" and smash your cone on the counter.

_____

You say, "Excuse me, there was a mistake. I paid for two scoops but you've given me only one."

_____

You say nothing and walk out the door feeling disappointed and angry.

_____

You get only a mediocre review at your part-time library job where you think you work very hard and conscientiously.

You curse at your supervisor. You tell her that your parents are on the city council and she could lose her job for evaluating you unfairly.

_____

You sulk and think that you must be a terrible worker and all-around stupid person and probably deserve the poor review.

_____

You approach your supervisor and ask if she can meet with you later to discuss your review. At the meeting you explain how you always try to work hard and efficiently and how surprised you were at receiving the mediocre review.

_____

You are working on a group science project. The group is deciding what each member will contribute to the project.

You say, "Let's talk about our strengths and how we can work together to do a good project. I'm good at doing research."

You let someone else tell you what you should do, and you don't say anything when they give you something you're not good at and really don't like doing.

Without asking for input, you tell the group what each person will do.

You would like to ask someone to dance but are afraid of rejection.

You walk up to someone who looks friendly and say, "Hi, would you like to dance?"

You stand by the wall, feeling angry that no one is asking you to dance.

You walk over to a group of kids, pull one forcefully by the arm and say, "Come on, dance with me."

now try this

Tell whether you are most often passive, assertive, or aggressive.

_____

Describe anything you may have missed out on at times you were passive.

_____

_____

_____

Tell what you could have done to be assertive instead.

_____

_____

_____

Describe anyone you may have hurt by being aggressive.

_____

_____

_____

Tell what you could have done to be assertive instead.

_____

_____

_____

Explain why being assertive might be difficult for you.

_____

_____

_____

_____

Describe how learning to be assertive could help you have healthier self-esteem.

_____

_____

_____

_____

As you go through the next few days, look for chances to practice being assertive. If you aren't sure what assertive behavior might be in some situation, ask a counselor or other adult for an opinion. Describe what happened when you tried to be assertive.

_____

_____

_____

_____

today's affirmation

I act assertively to create positive relationships and successful outcomes, which in turn build healthy self-esteem.

don't take everything personally 27

know this

Everyone has thoughts, feelings, and experiences that affect how they interact with others. Since we don't always know how someone's current personal state is affecting their words or actions, it's possible to misread them. We may take something personally that actually has nothing to do with us. This can affect our self-esteem.

Healthy self-esteem means you understand that other people's thoughts and actions aren't always related to you. For example, if your cousin doesn't comment on your new haircut it doesn't have to mean she doesn't like it; it might mean she's distracted by an argument she just had with her parents. Or if your friend doesn't invite you to watch a movie, it doesn't have to mean he's mad at you; it might just mean he wants some time alone.

This concept works the other way too. If you're worrying about your grandfather's illness and forget to meet your friends at the mall, it's not a personal message to them; it's because issues in your family overshadowed your social life. Your friends shouldn't take it personally or think you're mad at them.

When you believe that every time someone ignores you or is impolite to you it's because there's something wrong with you, you'll feel bad about yourself your whole life. All people have daily personal challenges that distract them and consume their time and energy. They carry their own needs and concerns with them just as you do.

try this

When Sophia texts Aisha and Aisha doesn't text her back right away, Sophia starts to wonder what's wrong. She tells herself Aisha is mad at her or trying to avoid her. She wonders if Aisha doesn't want to be friends anymore, and worries Aisha will tell others that Sophia isn't fun or caring. Sophia's self-esteem is affected negatively by her thinking.

List some other reasons that Aisha might not have texted Sophia back right away.

_____

_____

What could Sophia have told herself about the situation that wouldn't have made her feel bad about herself?

_____

_____

What else could Sophia have done instead of worrying about Aisha being mad at her?

_____

_____

When Riya leaves a message for Aisha and Aisha doesn't call her back right away, Riya doesn't take it personally or worry. She tells herself Aisha is probably busy and will get back to her when she has time. Riya goes on with her life and her self-esteem remains intact.

Do you think you more often respond like Sophia or like Riya? _____

now try this

Describe something that happened to you recently where you took it personally and felt your self-esteem dip.

_____

_____

_____

_____

_____

Answer these questions about the incident you described:

Do I know for sure this was a personal comment or action toward me?

_____

What is my proof that it was a personal message to me?

_____

_____

_____

What are at least two other possible reasons this could have been done or said that were not personal?

_____

_____

_____

_____

If I asked two other people, would they agree this was meant personally?

_____

Is there someone else I can check this out with?

_____

Am I willing to check it out with the person who said or did it?

_____

At http://www.newharbinger.com/50003, you can download and print copies of this exercise. In the next two weeks, when someone does or says something that you take personally and you feel your self-esteem dip again, repeat the exercise and record your answers on the worksheets you've printed.

Important Note: Even if you never find out for sure how someone's words or actions were meant, going through this question list will help you break the automatic thinking habit of taking everything personally and help you maintain healthy self-esteem.

today's affirmation

I check things out before taking words or actions personally because I know they aren't always about me.

no one is liked by everyone 28

---

know this

Sometimes we base our worth on how many people like us. This may be how many people want to connect with us in person or how many "likes" we get on social media. In either case, this accounting ultimately damages our self-esteem because there will always be someone who may not want to be friends with us. This isn't because there's something wrong with us, but just because being liked by every single other person is an impossible standard to meet.

When you think you're good enough only if everyone likes you, you're basing your self-worth on a false belief. As we've already established, every person has unconditional intrinsic value. And it's realistically impossible to be liked by *everyone*. Even if you try to be everything everyone else wants, there will be someone who doesn't like you for doing that! You yourself probably don't like all the people you meet, but that doesn't mean there's something wrong with them; it just means you don't click. It doesn't affect their value as human beings, and it doesn't affect yours if someone doesn't like you.

Trying to get every single person to like you is an unachievable goal. It keeps you running on a never-ending treadmill that only exhausts you and denies your authentic self. As long as you strive for this, you'll never feel good about yourself. The wiser, more realistic perspective is to understand that it's both okay and normal not to be liked by everyone. This perspective builds healthy self-esteem that, in turn, makes you a more likeable person!

try this

Fill in the chart below with your most favorite and least favorite colors, foods, clothes, and activities.

	Most favorite	Least favorite
Color		
Food		
Clothes		
Activity		

Does an item being on your "most favorite" list give it more value in the world?

_____

Does an item being on your "least favorite" list make it less valuable in the world?

_____

Tell what you think the author J.K. Rowling meant when she wrote the following words for the character Albus Dumbledore to speak in *Harry Potter and the Goblet of Fire*:

"Really, Hagrid, if you are holding out for universal popularity, I'm afraid you will be in this cabin for a very long time," said Dumbledore, now peering sternly over his half-moon spectacles. "Not a week has passed since I became Headmaster of this school, when I haven't had at least one owl complaining about the way I run it. But what should I do? Barricade myself in my study and refuse to talk to anybody?"

_____

_____

now try this

Using this chart, write down the names of people you've been worried about getting to like you. Rate each person on a 1 (low) to 10 (high) scale of how important you think it is for them to like you, and then tell how your life would change if they liked you.

Name	How important is it for them to like me?	How would my life change if they liked me?

List the things that would still be wonderful in your life even if you never got them to like you.

_____

_____

_____

_____

_____

Write a conscious decision to be okay with letting this go and moving on with your life.

_____

_____

_____

_____

_____

The next time you see these people, smile and silently wish them well. Then focus on the friends you do have and create healthy self-esteem.

today's affirmation

It's impossible for anyone to be liked by everyone! I recognize that reality and release this impossible goal.

know this

When friends try to talk you into thinking, feeling, or acting a certain way, it's called peer pressure. People do this to feel better about themselves. When people have healthy self-esteem they don't need to pressure others. When people have healthy self-esteem they don't need to give in to peer pressure.

When some kids at school learned that Aiden's parents would be away for the weekend, they urged him to have a party. Aiden's older sister, Brooke, was supposed to "watch" him, but Brooke would be working the overnight shift at her job. Aiden had never taken advantage of his family and didn't want to lose their trust. But everyone told him he shouldn't worry. They said his parents would never find out.

Aiden didn't know what to do. Some of the popular kids who never talked to him were asking him to invite them. As word got around, kids he didn't even know were asking about the party. It felt awesome to have so many people paying attention to him.

Aiden talked to his best friends, Matais and Anna. Matais said, "Don't let people push you around. Do what you really want to do." That was the problem—Aiden really wanted all these kids to keep liking him, and he wanted to keep his parents' trust too. But everyone kept saying they'd never find out, so maybe it didn't matter. "I'll be your friend either way," said Anna. "Do what you want."

try this

Tell what you think Aiden should do and why.

_____

_____

_____

_____

If Aiden has the party, who will be his friends that night?

_____

If Aiden doesn't have the party, who will be his friends that night?

_____

If Aiden has the party, who will be his friends two weeks afterward?

_____

If Aiden doesn't have the party, who will be his friends two weeks afterward?

_____

Tell who you think has healthy self-esteem in this story and why.

_____

_____

_____

_____

now try this

Circle any of the following that describe things you have felt pressured to do. Check any you have pressured others to do. (You may have both a circle and a check mark for some items.)

_____ gossip   _____ dress a certain way

_____ smoke or vape   _____ like or not like certain people

_____ drink   _____ watch certain videos or movies

_____ join a certain club   _____ take certain classes

_____ do drugs   _____ wear a certain hairstyle

_____ steal   _____ listen to particular music

_____ have a certain body size   _____ use certain sexual behaviors

_____ follow a particular religion   _____ get tattoos or piercings

_____ play certain sports   _____ use social media inappropriately

Describe one of the situations you circled. How healthy was your self-esteem in this situation?

_____

_____

_____

_____

Describe one of the situations you checked. How healthy was your self-esteem in this situation?

_____

_____

_____

_____

Peer pressure from others works when it feels too hard to stand up for ourselves. Picture yourself in a peer-pressure situation you have actually encountered. Circle the words you could say if it happens again, or write your own.

"No thanks, that's not for me."   "No, I don't want to."

"No thank you."   "No thanks, I'm not into that."

"No thanks, I'll pass."   _____

"No, I don't do that."   _____

"No, I'd rather not."   _____

"No thanks, not my style."   _____

today's affirmation

I have the strength to stand up to peer pressure;
I decide what's right for me.

setting healthy boundaries

---

know this

Setting healthy boundaries in relationships means putting limits on any kind of abusive behavior: physical, emotional, verbal, sexual, financial, digital, or stalking. Setting appropriate limits with other people helps you protect and respect yourself and contributes to healthy self-esteem.

When Destiny's friend Samantha continued to talk behind her back and share her personal information even though Destiny had asked her not to, Destiny felt angry and hurt. She didn't want to lose Samantha's friendship but she didn't like being betrayed. She stopped spending time with Samantha because she knew she could find a friend who would be loyal and respect her.

Kaylee felt cool dating Daniel because he was popular. But she didn't like him pushing her to experiment with substances more than she wanted to and being rude and harsh if she didn't comply. Kaylee felt conflicted but she broke up with Daniel because she refused to be disrespected. She knew she'd feel worse about herself if she stayed.

try this

The following behaviors can help people set healthy boundaries. Add more of your own on the blank lines.

Speaking up for yourself

Saying no to behaviors you're not comfortable with

Asking for a change in behaviors

Limiting the types of activities you do with someone

Distancing yourself from someone who is taking advantage of you

Blocking someone on your device or social media

Leaving a relationship that's threatening or harmful to you

Telling someone else how another person is treating you

Limiting the amount of time you spend with someone

_____

_____

_____

Tell how you already use any of these behaviors to set healthy boundaries.

_____

_____

_____

_____

_____

Which other behaviors do you think would be helpful for you to try?

_____

_____

_____

How does it feel to think about setting limits with other people?

_____

_____

_____

What would be the easiest part about setting limits for you?

_____

_____

_____

What would be the hardest part?

_____

_____

_____

How do you think setting limits would affect your self-esteem?

_____

_____

_____

now try this

Write your name in the middle of the circle below, leaving two or three inches between your name and the border of the circle. Imagine this circle is your protective healthy boundary. Inside the circle, write the names of people who treat you with respect. Outside the circle, write the names of anyone who doesn't treat you with respect or with whom you need to set a limit.

Tell how each of the people outside the circle treat you inappropriately and why you need to set limits with them.

_____

_____

_____

Write some ideas of how you can set limits with these people. You can use ideas from the previous list, or you can add more that are specific to the situation.

_____

_____

_____

Write a commitment to yourself to take action on setting a limit in the next week.

_____

_____

_____

After you've set the healthy boundary, describe the experience.

_____

_____

_____

How did taking action affect your self-esteem?

_____

_____

_____

today's affirmation

I set healthy boundaries with others and don't continue relationships where I'm abused or disrespected.

31 the look of healthy self-esteem

know this

When you feel good about yourself it shows physically. You sit or stand taller, smile more, look less stressed and move in a more confident way. Even when you're not completely confident, having the look of healthy self-esteem can help you feel it. This look sends the social signal that you're happy, open, and want to connect. Your look is inviting, and people are attracted to your cheerfulness and positivity.

Dylan's family moved a lot because his dad was in the army, and Dylan often felt nervous starting at a new school. He wondered how people would respond to him, whether he'd make friends, and what the kids would be like. From making so many new starts, Dylan learned he'd feel more confident if he looked and acted with confidence. So on the first day Dylan always wore his favorite jeans and a comfortable shirt that fit well. He worked out before school to release anxiety. He ate a good breakfast so his stomach wouldn't growl. And before he entered the building he'd mentally affirm to himself that he was a friendly person and would meet other friendly people that day. He made it a point to walk tall and smile. It took some concentration and energy, but this plan always worked for Dylan. When he looked the part of healthy self-esteem, that's what he felt inside.

try this

The following attributes are generally those of people who have healthy self-esteem. Exhibiting these characteristics can help you look and feel more positive and confident in yourself.

Rate each attribute from 1 (low) to 10 (high) according to how much you think you exhibit this already. Circle any of those you'd like to work on improving.

Clean clothes _____   Open look on face _____

Clean body _____   Looking into people's eyes
                             when you talk to them _____
Positive attitude _____
                             Good posture _____
Smile _____
                             Speaking clearly _____
Happy look on face _____
                             Relaxed and stable character _____

List the names of three people you know who you think have healthy self-esteem.

Tell which of the above attributes they exhibit.

_____

_____

_____

What other attributes do you see that make them look confident about themselves?

_____

_____

_____

now try this

Choose one day this week to try an experiment. When you wake up in the morning, imagine you already have solid, healthy self-esteem and then act on that premise for the rest of the day. Go through each situation as if you feel confident in yourself and your relationships, you're happy to be alive, and you like your authentic self. Set the intention that all day in every situation with every person you will act as if the healthy self-esteem you want is already yours. You'll show it in your eyes and your smile, in the way you walk and talk. Today you'll feel the peace and happiness that comes from genuinely accepting yourself, both strengths and weaknesses combined. Try to keep this attitude and behavior as you go through the day. (And remember it's okay if you slip up! If that happens, just notice it and get back on track.)

After your experiment, describe what it was like to do this.

_____

_____

_____

_____

When did you feel most comfortable?

_____

_____

When did you feel most uncomfortable?

_____

_____

What did you like best about this experiment?

_____

_____

What did you like least about this experiment?

_____

_____

Tell about any ways this experiment made your self-esteem go up, and also any ways it made your self-esteem go down.

_____

_____

_____

_____

_____

_____

_____

today's affirmation

When I look and act confident and friendly, it helps me
feel confident and friendly.

32 the power of managing feelings

know this

All feelings are okay. It's what you do with them that will either help or hurt you. When you're aware of your feelings you can learn to manage them in a healthy way.

Nikki couldn't sit still. Her stomach had butterflies, and it was hard to focus in health class. Ms. Elsbury, her health teacher, asked what was wrong. Nikki didn't answer, but her eyes filled with tears. She felt embarrassed and looked away.

"What's going on?" Ms. Elsbury asked when they were in her office.

"I don't want to talk about it," said Nikki.

"If we don't let feelings out, they actually get bigger," said Ms. Elsbury.

"Well, I don't want that," said Nikki. She told Ms. Elsbury that her mom was in the hospital. Her dad visited there every evening while she took care of her younger sisters. Nikki was worried about her mom and wasn't able to concentrate or keep up with homework.

"I'm so sorry to hear this," said Ms. Elsbury. "What's the hardest part for you?"

"I'm afraid my mom won't get better," said Nikki. "But if I let myself feel that fear, I might cry and never stop."

"When we're afraid of feelings, we tend to push them away," said Ms. Elsbury. "But they don't go away; they're only hidden temporarily. When they resurface, they're even stronger. Let's look at a plan for managing feelings." Ms. Elsbury gave Nikki the following handout and read it with her.

Four-Step Plan for Managing Feelings

1. Name the feeling. What is it? Sadness, anger, joy, compassion, disappointment, embarrassment, disgust, shame, love?

2. Accept the feeling. It's always okay to feel your feelings! Remind yourself of this. Quietly to yourself or out loud, say: "It's okay to feel _____."

3. Express the feeling. Expressing a feeling is the only way to release it. It's important to express it in a way that doesn't hurt you or anyone else. Writing, speaking, physical movement, relaxation, crying, singing, and drawing can all be safe ways to express feelings.

4. Take care of yourself in a healthy way. What do you need right now to take care of yourself? A hug, a nap, a shower, a walk, a friend, a party, attention, compassion? You can give yourself whatever you need at the moment.

"I've never thought about what to do with feelings before," said Nikki.

"That's okay," said Ms. Elsbury. "It's something you can learn—just like you learned to add and spell and tie your shoes. Managing feelings is one of the most important skills we ever learn. It directly affects our success and happiness in every area of life. When we're confident in managing feelings, we have healthier self-esteem too."

try this

To become familiar with your feelings, make enough copies of the following chart to last a week. You can download it at http://www.newharbinger.com/50003. Then start paying attention to your feelings as you go through the days. Record what you observe. The list below may help you identify your feelings. You can also add any others that you experience. Remember, all feelings are okay, but expressing them should never hurt you or others.

abandoned	disappointed	betrayed
content	brave	frustrated
loving	anxious	apprehensive
stressed	lonely	thrilled
shocked	irritated	ashamed
guilty	jealous	relieved
excited	peaceful	relaxed
happy	worried	depressed
embarrassed	angry	_____
confused	sad	_____
surprised	afraid	_____

Day	What I feel	Where I notice it in my body	How I express it
Morning			
Afternoon			
Night			

now try this

When you consciously manipulate, or do something with, your feelings, you are taking charge of them. Try any or all of the following ways to work with your feelings. Use the blank lines to add your own ideas. Give yourself some time to complete this. After you try each activity, rate how well it worked for you (1 = ineffective to 10 = very effective.) Write your rating number next to the description of the activity.

After identifying your feeling:

_____   Say your feeling out loud: "I am feeling _____ right now."

_____   Write a paragraph or more about it.

_____   Describe it to someone you trust.

_____   Express it on paper without words, using color, line, texture, or form.

_____   If it fits with your feeling, cry it out.

_____   Write a letter to someone you are having feelings about. Do not send the letter.

_____   Write or draw your feeling and put the paper through a shredder.

_____   Write or draw your feeling and frame the paper.

_____   Write or draw your feeling and give the paper away to someone else.

_____   Write or draw your feeling and tear up the paper.

_____   Write or draw your feeling and crumple up the paper and throw it away.

_____   Write or draw your feeling on bathroom tissue and flush it away.

_____ Do some safe physical exercise—such as walking, swimming, or stretching—to release the energy of your feeling.

_____ Sing your feeling.

_____ Play out your feeling on an instrument.

_____ _____

_____ _____

_____ _____

_____ _____

_____ _____

today's affirmation

All my feelings are okay and I manage them in a healthy way.

33 tolerating discomfort

Jada felt discomfort because everyone else had dressed up for Anthony's party and she was wearing cut-off jeans. She was tempted to sneak out the back door, but she didn't really want to; she'd been looking forward to the party for weeks. Jada realized that her discomfort was about a fear of being rejected or made fun of. She decided to remember that it didn't matter what she wore—her real friends wouldn't care. A couple of kids teased her in a friendly way, and she laughed with them about it, but by the end of the night she'd proved herself right—her real friends didn't care. She felt good about herself for tolerating her discomfort.

Jeremiah felt discomfort at the football tryouts because it seemed everyone else was so much better than him. He changed his mind about trying out and rode home on the late bus. He went to his room and tried to do homework but he kept thinking about how much he'd wanted to make the team and how embarrassed he would feel when people asked him what happened. Jeremiah felt his self-esteem take a nosedive.

Mia felt discomfort about trusting Evelyn when they became friends. Mia had been hurt before when friends betrayed her. She told herself she wouldn't become close with anyone again. But Evelyn was so nice; they had a lot in common and had so much fun together. Part of Mia wanted to stop seeing Evelyn so the discomfort would go away and she'd feel safe again. Part of her wanted to tolerate the discomfort and hope that Evelyn wouldn't betray her. She didn't know what to do.

David won a free concert ticket in a giveaway contest. When he received his ticket, he found out he could get a second free ticket, but he'd have to drive to the arena and stand in a long line that would take about an hour. David wanted the second ticket so he could take a friend to the concert, but he would feel discomfort having to drive so far and stand in a boring line for so long with people he didn't know. He couldn't decide if he should get the second ticket or not.

try this

Circle the word or phrase that best describes how high your discomfort would have been if you were in Jada's situation. Then tell what you would have done in her place.

very low   low   medium   high   very high

_____

_____

Circle the word or phrase that best describes how high your discomfort would have been if you were in Jeremiah's situation. Then tell what you would have done in his place.

very low   low   medium   high   very high

_____

_____

Circle the word or phrase that best describes how high your discomfort would be if you were in Mia's situation. Then tell what you would have done in her place.

very low   low   medium   high   very high

_____

_____

Circle the word or phrase that best describes how high your discomfort would be if you were in David's situation. Then tell what you would have done in his place.

very low   low   medium   high   very high

_____

_____

now try this

Write a number from 1 (low) to 10 (high) next to each description to tell how strong your discomfort would be in this situation. Then describe what you might gain from tolerating the discomfort.

_____ *You are lifting weights to gain muscle strength, and you're bored only halfway through the workout.*

Benefit of tolerating the discomfort of continuing: _____

_____

_____

_____ *You are babysitting for neighbors, and they call to ask if you can stay two extra hours. They pay well and you need the money, but you're already eager to leave and meet your friends.*

Benefit of tolerating the discomfort of staying: _____

_____

_____

_____ *Your date, who has so far been fun and nice and interesting, suggests watching a TV show you can't stand.*

Benefit of tolerating the discomfort of watching: _____

_____

_____

_____ *You are home on a Friday night and feeling lonely. Some kids call and ask you to do something that would be fun but that you could get into trouble for.*

Benefit of tolerating the discomfort of loneliness: _____

_____

_____

_____ *Your parents are fighting again and you're feeling depressed. You've thought about running away before and tonight it feels like it might be the only answer.*

Benefit of tolerating the discomfort of staying: _____

_____

_____

_____ *You need to retake a class you failed in order to graduate. You hate the subject and don't get along with the teacher.*

Benefit of tolerating the discomfort of retaking the class: _____

_____

_____

Circle the situations in which you ever tolerated discomfort and gained something. Then write your own story of a time this happened.

learned to walk	studied for a test
went to a social event	helped a person in need
woke up earlier than you'd like	asked for help
did a boring task	tried a new activity
talked to someone new	got a cavity filled
admitted you were wrong	faced a fear

My story: _____

_____

_____

_____

_____

_____

Describe a current challenge in your life where you must decide whether or not you will tolerate discomfort. Tell what the benefits of tolerating the discomfort would be.

_____

_____

_____

_____

_____

_____

_____

_____

today's affirmation

I can tolerate discomfort and gain something from doing so.

the power of inner peace 34

know this

When we think and act from peace, that's what we bring to ourselves, our relationships, our goals and activities. Acting from peace helps create successes and builds healthy self-esteem.

When we're stressed we bring tension to every relationship, experience, situation, and challenge. Starting from stress means we're tired and discouraged before we even begin.

When we're at peace we bring peace to everything. Anything we attempt is easier to achieve when we approach it from peace. Inner stillness helps us think clearly and make positive choices. We're more patient with ourselves and others. We carry peace to every person and every situation.

Many people think inner peace is something we have to "get," but actually we already carry it within us. It's said that when the renowned artist Michelangelo was asked how he created the powerful statue of David from a solid piece of marble, he replied that he didn't—he said David was already in the stone; all he did was to chip away the excess rock and unearth him.

Like David at the core of the stone, there is peace at our core. It might be covered up with negative thoughts, but if we chip away at them we'll find serenity underneath. When we center ourselves in that core of peace, everything we say and do comes from peace. Whatever the outside circumstances, when we reconnect with the tranquility deep within us we access peace and create successes that build healthy self-esteem.

try this

Describe a time when you felt deeply peaceful. What helped you achieve this peace?

_____

_____

_____

_____

Describe a time when you felt very agitated. What brought you to that state?

_____

_____

_____

_____

Do you tend to feel better about yourself when you're at peace or when you're agitated?

_____

How does your level of inner peace affect your ability to make smart choices, think positively, and find success in what you're doing?

_____

_____

_____

_____

Check any of the following techniques that you already use to access your deep inner peace. Circle any more that you'd like to try. (Add more of your own on the blank lines.)

breathwork

mindfulness (staying grounded in the present moment)

meditation

acceptance of circumstances and people

belief in a higher power

calming activities

visualization

positive thinking

journaling

coloring

taking a walk

other exercise

peaceful music

being in nature

bath or shower

petting an animal

playing an instrument

reading for pleasure

_____

_____

_____

now try this

Make a commitment to do one of the above activities today or tomorrow. Record a realistic time frame here so you're sure to follow through.

_____

As you do the activity, let yourself enjoy feeling peaceful and relaxed. Focus on feeling calm in both your body and your mind, and affirm that you're releasing negativity and finding your inner core of peace.

What was the hardest part about trying this?

_____

What was the easiest part?

_____

Write some realistic short- and long-term goals for using calming techniques to access your inner peace. For example, you might start with one time per week and gradually increase to three, and then five.

_____

_____

_____

_____

_____

_____

_____

Which techniques do you think are the best fit for you personally?

_____

_____

Which techniques don't appeal to you at all?

_____

_____

Try a calming activity before making an important decision or facing a challenge. Describe what happens.

_____

_____

_____

_____

_____

_____

Remember, if the first activity you try doesn't work well, you can try another. Or you can switch them up each day for variety. The more you practice increasing your peace, the more calm you'll become and the more you'll find success and healthy self-esteem.

today's affirmation

I practice accessing my inner peace to build healthy self-esteem.

35 thinking habits that help or hinder

know this

Some thinking habits can make us feel negative about everything, including ourselves. Other thinking habits are more likely to create positive feelings about our lives and ourselves. Using the positive thinking habits keeps our self-esteem healthy.

You can use the acronym ABOP to help yourself remember four types of thinking habits that either help or hinder healthy self-esteem.

A = All-or-Nothing Thinking

All-or-nothing thinking is the tendency to judge things in extreme, or black-and-white, categories. This is irrational thinking because in reality things are never completely one way or the other. Thinking about yourself in this way *hinders* healthy self-esteem. For example, you may irrationally think that if you don't achieve perfection (which is impossible) you're a failure.

> *Mateo often scored the most goals in every soccer game. He thought of himself as an excellent player. But if he ever missed a goal he'd think,* Now I'm a total failure. *When he tried to help his mother wash some upper-story windows and the ladder scratched the side of the house Mateo told himself,* I'm worthless as a son. *This kind of all-or-nothing thinking caused Mateo's self-esteem to plummet every time he made a mistake.*

B = Bigger Picture

Sometimes people focus so closely on one or two small details of a situation that they lose sight of the bigger picture, or the whole context those details are in. Focusing on one small negative aspect of a situation or yourself can damage self-esteem. A healthier thinking habit is to see the bigger picture, or realize that one detail is always just part of a bigger unit and is far less significant when seen in comparison to the whole. This thinking habit *helps* healthy self-esteem.

Sarah had a part in the chorus for the school musical. She loved theater and was a good dancer. But on opening night she did a wrong turn and bumped into another chorus member, causing them both to trip. They were in the back and hardly anyone noticed, but Sarah felt terrible. She replayed the scene in her mind for hours, which made her self-esteem nose-dive, and she considered leaving the show. "This was a small mistake!" *the director told her.* "Stop focusing on one flaw and see the bigger picture. You did all the rest of the numbers beautifully—you're an asset to the show."

O = Overgeneralizing

When people overgeneralize, they assume that because they had one negative experience in the past they'll always have the same negative experience in the future— even though there's no evidence for that. This assumption is irrational and *hinders* healthy self-esteem. People who overgeneralize often use the words "always," "never," "no one," "everyone," "all," and "none."

When Lauren asked someone she liked to the school dance, they said no. She thought, No one will ever want to date me; I'm always being rejected. *Her self-esteem started to suffer anytime she was with someone she was attracted to. More rationally she could have thought,* Just because one person turned me down doesn't mean everyone else will.

P = Positivity

It's easy for our brains to grasp on to negative thoughts when something goes wrong. But the longer we let them dwell there, the harder it is to feel good again. One negative thought leads to another, and then a downward spiral begins. The sooner we pull our minds out of the negative and into the positive, the sooner we can start feeling better about ourselves. Focusing on the positive *helps* healthy self-esteem.

Harlow frequently let their thinking get into a negative rut, and it was often about themself. One day their aunt sent them a recording of positive affirmations. They realized that these thoughts were the exact opposite of what they were thinking when they felt down on themself. They started listening to the affirmations regularly and stuck a couple on their mirror. The more they took in the positive thoughts, the less they fell into the downward spiral of low self-esteem.

try this

The kids in the descriptions below are using thinking habits that hinder healthy self-esteem. Identify which thinking habit each person is using, and then tell how they could change their thinking to feel better about themselves.

Francisco is trying to get fit for the wrestling season. He's lifting weights regularly, eating less junk food and more fruits and vegetables, and drinking protein shakes. He feels stronger and more focused than ever. One day he has a large ice cream sundae with his friends and has a bad workout the next day. I stink at self-discipline and training, *he tells himself.* I may as well quit now!

_____

_____

_____

_____

Ethan is nervous about being the first one to give his oral presentation in history class. He already has a solid B in the class, is well-prepared, has good visual aids, and has a good relationship with the teacher. But Ethan's self-esteem is dipping because he thinks having to go first will trip him up.

_____

_____

_____

_____

When Bailey drops her lunch tray in the school cafeteria, which has never happened before, she tells herself, It figures; I'm such a klutz. I'm always causing accidents. *When she babysits for the first time, the baby has an earache and won't stop crying. Bailey tells herself,* I'll never be good with kids. I'll make a terrible mother. *Bailey's self-esteem is low when she thinks this way.*

_____

_____

_____

_____

Alexa wakes up in the morning and thinks about how poorly she's doing in Spanish. She dreads going to school to face that class. She gets dressed and worries that her clothes are a bit out of style. She thinks she looks stupid. She checks her social media and sees that her friend Tanya has a new boyfriend. Alexa thinks about how she hasn't had a date all year. Alexa starts out her day with low self-esteem.

_____

_____

_____

_____

now try this

For the next few days pay attention to your thinking habits and keep a record of statements you use that fall into the ABOP categories. At http://www.newharbinger .com/50003, you'll find a form you can download for this exercise.

All-or-Nothing Thinking _____

_____

_____

Bigger Picture _____

_____

_____

Overgeneralizing _____

_____

_____

Positivity _____

_____

_____

Which habits that help healthy self-esteem do you use the most?

_____

_____

Which habits that hinder healthy self-esteem do you use the most?

_____

_____

What patterns do you see as to when, where, or in what situations you help your self-esteem?

_____

_____

What patterns do you see as to when, where, or in what situations you hinder your self-esteem?

_____

_____

Which habit or habits would you most like to work on improving?

_____

_____

Write some statements that would help your self-esteem.

_____

_____

_____

today's affirmation

I choose thinking habits that help, not hinder, my healthy self-esteem.

36 accepting mistakes

know this

Every human being is imperfect, including you. Perfection is literally impossible, and you, like everyone else, are set up to make mistakes. You will continue making mistakes as long as you are alive. This has nothing to do with your worth.

When Jack heard the buzzer, he wished he could disappear through the gym floor. He had missed the final shot and lost the division game for his team. For the whole school. For the whole town! He walked off the court and into the locker room, hoping to leave before anyone found him.

As the rest of his team came in, they patted Jack on the back and congratulated him on a good game. "Don't worry. We've got next year," one said. But he could sense their disappointment. He hated himself for letting them down. He picked up his duffel bag without bothering to shower or change. He just had to get out of there.

He heard Coach Anderson call, "Hey Jack, let's talk."

"I really don't want to," Jack said. "I feel bad enough already."

"Then just listen," said Coach. He told Jack a story of how in college he had missed the same shot in the playoffs and felt like he could never face his team again.

"You?" Jack said. "But you're a fantastic player and an awesome coach!"

"We all mess up sometimes. Making mistakes is part of being human. Ever notice that every keyboard has a delete key? They don't just hand those out to certain people. Everyone gets them, automatically, because everyone makes mistakes.

"If you choose to see each mistake as a normal part of life, and a chance to learn and grow, you automatically turn it into something positive. As the story goes, when Thomas Edison tried over 900 times to create a working light bulb, someone asked him how he felt about his failures. Edison said, 'I didn't fail—I just found 899 ways not to make a light bulb.'"

try this

On a separate sheet of paper, keep a record of human beings you see making mistakes. Maybe your little brother trips when he's running; maybe your dad spills his coffee; maybe you see a car accident. Human mistakes are boundless. See how long it takes you to witness a hundred mistakes, including your own.

now try this

Change your thoughts to change your feelings about yourself. First, make a list of any negative thoughts you have when you make a mistake.

_____

_____

_____

_____

Now cross out those statements and write new, positive thoughts that will help you accept imperfection and feel better about yourself.

_____

_____

_____

_____

Think about a mistake you made recently that you got down on yourself for. Close your eyes, take a few cleansing breaths, and relax. Now picture yourself making that same mistake, but responding with healthy self-esteem. Imagine what you would do and say differently. Imagine treating yourself with the compassion and rational thinking that is part of healthy self-esteem. Write this story on a separate piece of paper or in your phone, and read it over whenever you need to remember that mistakes are okay.

today's affirmation

My goal is not to stop making mistakes; my goal is to use them to learn and grow.

the power of gratitude

---

know this

Gratitude is an attitude of thankfulness and appreciation. When we practice an attitude of gratitude, we give attention to and celebrate all that is good in our life and in ourselves. This raises our level of happiness and peace, both about our circumstances and about ourselves, which then contributes to healthy self-esteem.

Alex felt like he was stuck in a rut. He hated getting out of bed in the morning to hear his parents nagging him to do his chores. He hated sitting through classes, listening to boring teachers. He hated going to work after school, stocking shelves and having to be nice to customers he didn't even know. He hated sitting in his room at night, pretending to do homework he didn't care about. The only time Alex felt happy was when he was with his girlfriend, Leah. But lately even Leah couldn't get him out of his bad mood.

"I'm getting tired of this," Leah told him. "All you do is talk about what's bad. I don't want to hear any more about your awful parents, your awful classes, or your awful job. Your life isn't that terrible, Alex. You just don't appreciate what you've got. And I don't think you appreciate me anymore, either. Maybe we shouldn't hang out together so much."

"Wait," said Alex. "I'm sorry I'm so down. I just can't find any reason to feel happy. I don't want to lose you, but I don't know how to change my life."

"You don't have to change your life," said Leah. "You just have to change your attitude. Instead of complaining, start being grateful. Focus on the good. Be glad you even have parents—you could be an orphan. Be glad you're healthy and can go to school—there's a kid in a hospital somewhere right now who would give anything to sit in one of your boring classes. Be glad you have a job so you can put gas in your car and go to the mall and the movies!"

"You're right," said Alex. "When you put it like that, I realize I do have a lot to be grateful for. I wish I could keep that attitude."

"Just continue to focus on all the good in your life," said Leah. "You'll feel happier, and you'll be a lot nicer to be around."

try this

Like Alex, many of us take a lot for granted. We forget about what we are fortunate to have. There are many people who don't have the things listed below. Think about what it would be like without any of these, and circle those you are grateful for.

sense of sight	bed to sleep in	ability to read
place to live	ability to speak	education
food in the refrigerator	freedom of speech	functioning brain
friends	sense of taste	ability to love
sense of hearing	family	ability to breathe on your own

Finish the following sentences:

I am grateful for _____

I feel fortunate because _____

One thing I really appreciate is _____

Something I will always be thankful for is _____

Try to identify and be grateful for the good in you. Tell three things you are grateful for about yourself in each of the following categories.

Physical

1. _____

2. _____

3. _____

Mental/Emotional

1. _____

2. _____

3. _____

Spiritual

1. _____

2. _____

3. _____

now try this

For the next week, pay attention to the good in your life. Every night before you go to sleep, write down five things you were grateful for that day; you'll find a worksheet for this at http://www.newharbinger.com/50003. These could be anything from "I was able to get out of bed," to "I won the track relay," to "It was a sunny day." Continue to think of more as you fall asleep.

Day 1

1. _____

2. _____

3. _____

4. _____

5. _____

Day 2

1. _____

2. _____

3. _____

4. _____

5. _____

Day 3

1. _____

2. _____

3. _____

4. _____

5. _____

Day 4

1. _____

2. _____

3. _____

4. _____

5. _____

Day 5

1. _____

2. _____

3. _____

4. _____

5. _____

Day 6

1. _____

2. _____

3. _____

4. _____

5. _____

Day 7

1. _____

2. _____

3. _____

4. _____

5. _____

At the end of the week, describe how focusing on the good in your life affected you.

today's affirmation

I focus on all the good in my life.

---

know this

Your life is limited only by your thoughts. When you can see the infinite possibilities present in every moment, situation, and person, you have the ability to grow, change, and become anything you desire.

Josh was fishing with his Uncle Brian. The conversation turned to the family business, and Josh complained that his dad expected him to join the business someday, but he had no interest in it. He also had no interest in his classes, his after-school job, or being on the basketball team. He felt trapped in his life and sometimes felt like running away.

Uncle Brian asked why Josh didn't make some changes. "That's impossible," Josh said. "Dad expects me to go into the business because I'm the oldest. I have to take certain classes to get into college—except I'd rather go to the police academy. I have to work at a fast-food job because I don't have any other experience. And I can't quit basketball because I've played since grade school."

"That's a lot of 'have-tos' and 'can'ts,'" said Uncle Brian. "It seems you're seeing life from a very narrow perspective. That's really limiting."

"What do you mean?" asked Josh. "How could I see it differently?"

"Instead of seeing traps, see possibilities," said Uncle Brian. "Talk to your dad, and explain what you'd really like to do with your future. Change your classes and get on a track to prepare for police work. Apply for new jobs and see what happens. Try a new sport—or take a break from sports for a while."

"But I feel stuck," said Josh. "Nothing will ever change."

"You're stuck only in your thinking," said Uncle Brian. "The truth is that each moment offers infinite possibilities. We decided to fish today, but that could change at any time. We could decide to go home right now or we could lie down on the pier and nap. I could push you into the water and jump in after you and we could both go swimming.

"It might feel like you're trapped by your family, your experiences, or your personality—but in reality, you're only trapped by your thoughts. If you believe you have choices you'll begin to see them. When we open our minds to infinite possibilities we can expand and grow, and choose any path we want from the millions before us."

try this

List ten things you do in an average day. After each, list a different choice you could make. It doesn't have to be something you would actually do, but just open your mind to new possibilities. For example, if you usually get out of bed on the right side, you could exit at the foot. If you usually say "hi," you could say "hey" or "hello." Let your mind practice thinking differently.

Regular Activity	Alternate Choice

Circle one or more thoughts you feel trapped in from the list below or write your own. Then open your mind, and write a different thought you could choose instead.

"I'm a loser." _____

_____

"I can't change." _____

_____

"I'm bad." _____

_____

"I'm stupid." _____

_____

"I can't do anything right." _____

_____

"I'll never be good enough." _____

_____

Other: _____

_____

_____

_____

_____

_____

now try this

Opening your mind is like opening a door. The wider you open it, the more you see.

Stand at the door of the room you're in now. Open the door one inch, just enough to see past it. List the items you see in the space beyond.

_____

_____

Open the door six inches. Count how many more items you can see.

_____

_____

Open the door three feet. Count how many more items you can see now.

_____

_____

Make a list of situations you feel trapped in.

_____

_____

Choose one item from your list and describe it from a trapped perspective—with the door of your mind open only an inch.

_____

_____

_____

Open the door of your mind six inches. Describe the new possibilities you see.

_____

_____

_____

Open the door of your mind three feet. Describe the possibilities you see now.

_____

_____

_____

If possibilities were limitless, what would you do differently tomorrow?

_____

_____

Next week?

_____

_____

_____

Next year?

_____

_____

_____

If possibilities were limitless, how would you choose to think about yourself?

_____

_____

_____

today's affirmation

I can choose from limitless possibilities at every moment.

39 the power of conviction

know this

Conviction is a strong belief and certitude. When you believe deeply in yourself and your goals, you gain the strength to get through challenges, to follow your dreams, and to remain true to yourself.

Andrea had been through a lot. She was born with a number of heart problems that required multiple surgeries before she was five and prevented her from participating in many activities. Her father had walked out when things got too hard, and her mother took a second job to support Andrea and her sister, Melanie. Andrea and Melanie were often alone after school when they were young because their mom couldn't afford day care or a babysitter. On those afternoons they would video chat with Grandma Jen, who would help them with homework, encourage them, share her wisdom, or sometimes just tell funny stories to make them laugh.

Grandma Jen had experienced a lot in her own life. She dropped out of eighth grade to take care of her younger sisters after her mother was killed in an accident. Once her sisters were grown, she finally got her high school certificate and met Grandpa Johnny. They had two children before he was drafted into the military. The war depressed Johnny, and he turned to alcohol to cope. When he came home, Grandma Jen stood by him as he went through treatment and recovery from addiction.

"There will always be challenges in life," Grandma Jen would tell Andrea and Melanie. "Since we can't get rid of them, we have to learn how to handle them. One of the most important things you can do when times get hard is to never give up! You might have challenges with friends, school, health, or family—and maybe even all at once. You might feel like people have pushed you down and each time you try to stand up they push you down again. But if you have the conviction that you can make it, you can."

try this

Imagine that the outline of the body in this frame represents you. Fill it in or decorate it to show yourself filled with strength and conviction. Use colors, lines, forms, or textures that depict an unwavering belief in yourself.

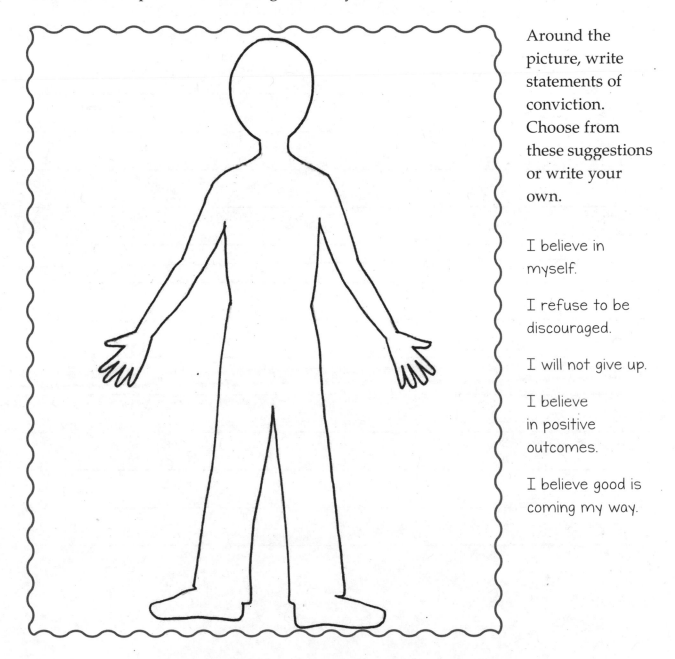

Around the picture, write statements of conviction. Choose from these suggestions or write your own.

I believe in myself.

I refuse to be discouraged.

I will not give up.

I believe in positive outcomes.

I believe good is coming my way.

now try this

List anything you have accomplished in your life. These achievements could be mental, physical, or spiritual; they could relate to family, friends, school, or activities. Put a star next to those that were the hardest to attain. Tell how your life would have been different if you had given up before you achieved these goals.

_____

_____

_____

_____

_____

_____

_____

_____

_____

_____

_____

Choose one of the items you starred to use in the picture below. Write your accomplishment on the line under the picture. Draw yourself at the start of the obstacle course. Write or draw your accomplishment at the end of the course. At each obstacle, write or draw something you had to overcome to reach your goal. (For example, if your accomplishment was passing an English class, your obstacles might have been tests, papers, or a teacher who was a hard grader.)

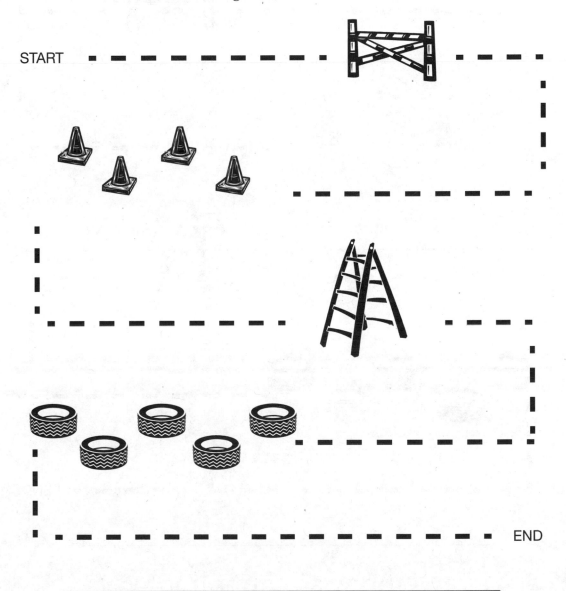

START

END

_____

Title the bottom of the next picture with the name of a current challenge you are facing. Draw yourself at the start of the obstacle course. Write or draw your goal at the end of the course. At each obstacle, write or draw something that might make it hard for you to reach your goal.

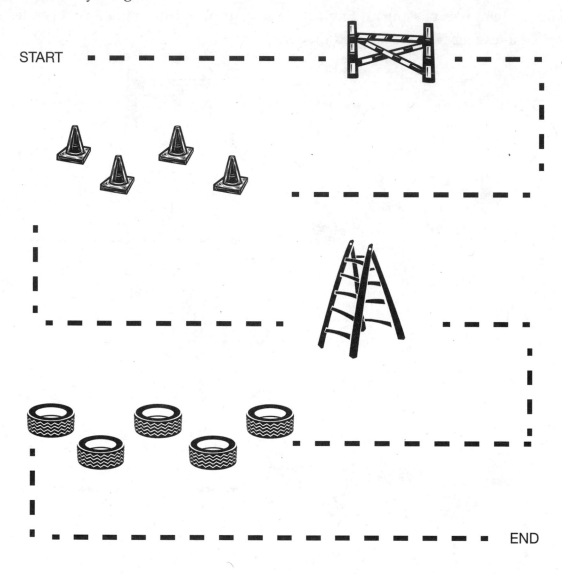

START

END

today's affirmation

I refuse to give up! I refuse to be discouraged!

the power of responsibility 40

---

know this

Blaming other people or external circumstances for what your life is like gives away your power and leads to negativity and helplessness. Accepting responsibility for your life means you are in charge of your thoughts, feelings, and actions. It gives you back your power and lets you grow into your authentic self.

Mr. Hernandez, James's English teacher, asked James to stay after class. James had always been a good writer and an A student in English, but his last few papers had been late, and he had stopped participating in class—when he bothered to show up. Mr. Hernandez asked whether anything was wrong.

"A lot," said James. "I didn't make the volleyball team because the coach is way too picky about skills. And my mom is marrying this guy I hardly know. I'm feeling really angry at these people for ruining my life, and now they're ruining my grades too."

"Those things sound hard," said Mr. Hernandez. "I don't blame you for feeling upset. But it sounds like you're blaming other people for your lack of happiness and success."

"Well, it is their fault," said James. "If the coach were more reasonable, I would have made the team. If my mom weren't doing something stupid, I could concentrate more on school."

"When we don't like something about our life," said Mr. Hernandez, "it might feel easier to blame someone else. Then we don't have to do anything to change. But blaming makes us powerless victims. It also creates unhealthy self-esteem, because deep down inside we know our happiness is our job, not someone else's."

"But Coach and Mom aren't going to change their minds—and what they're doing affects me a lot. I am powerless over them!" said James.

"So take back your power," said Mr. Hernandez. "Ask the coach what you can do differently to make the team next year, and then improve and show him what you can do. Let your mother know how you feel, and then decide you're not going to let her choices affect your happiness. Take responsibility for your own actions and feelings. Blaming leads to negativity and helplessness. Taking responsibility lets you grow into your authentic self and your true potential."

187

try this

Fiona was caught smoking cigarettes and was suspended from school. She blamed her older brother because he had given her the cigarettes.

How could Fiona take back her power?

_____

Gavin failed his history test. He blamed the teacher because she hadn't given the class a study guide.

How could Gavin take back his power?

_____

Jemma was grounded because she got home late three nights in a row past her 10:00 p.m. curfew. She blamed her parents because the curfew was too early.

How could Jemma take back her power?

_____

Angel was mad at Evan for sharing a secret that Angel had told him not to share. Evan blamed Angel for telling him the secret in the first place.

How could Evan take back his power?

_____

London has low self-esteem. She blames her parents for being too critical.

How could London take back her power?

_____

now try this

Put a B next to any situations that describe times you feel like blaming someone else for your actions.

_____   I stub my toe.

_____   I drop my books.

_____   I trip on the sidewalk or in the hall.

_____   I receive a low grade on a test or paper.

_____   I spill my drink.

_____   I get into trouble for arguing with my sibling.

_____   I feel angry.

_____   I bump into someone.

_____   I forget to do my chores.

_____   I sleep through my alarm.

_____   I miss the ball when playing a sport.

_____   I forget my homework.

_____   I lose my homework.

_____   My bedroom is messy.

_____   I accidentally break a window, lamp, or other property.

_____   I am late for class.

_____   I go over the limit on my cell phone minutes.

Circle anything that is your responsibility. Add more of your own.

my feelings	my schoolwork
my actions	what I say
how I feel about myself	what I think
my job	how I treat my body
my beliefs	_____
how I treat other people	_____
how I treat myself	_____
my chores	_____

Name the people you tend to blame for your unhappiness.

At home: _____

_____

At school: _____

_____

With friends: _____

_____

You may have learned where your unhealthy self-esteem came from. This is understanding, not blaming. Once you understand, it is your job to do the repair work. Describe what you can do to take responsibility for creating healthier self-esteem.

What thoughts do you need to change?

_____

_____

_____

_____

_____

What behaviors do you need to change?

_____

_____

_____

_____

_____

On a separate sheet of paper, write a letter to someone you have blamed. Tell that person you are taking back your power. (Decide whether or not you will really send this letter.)

today's affirmation

I keep my power by taking responsibility for my actions.

41 the power of positive decisions

know this

Positive decisions are those that will most likely result in positive outcomes. When you make a positive decision, even if it is not the easiest one to follow through on, you create a better chance of having a positive outcome.

Jemal's little brother had been caught copying a report from the internet instead of writing it himself. He was also starting to hang around kids who had bad reputations. Jemal was concerned and asked him what was going on.

"It was so much easier to copy that paper than do it myself," his brother said. "I'm not good at writing. And I know I might get into trouble with those kids, but it's fun to do risky stuff—it feels cool."

"It might have seemed easier to copy the paper," Jemal said, "but then look what happened—you were suspended for a day and had to rewrite the report and Mom and Dad grounded you. Your decision seemed positive at first but it wasn't, because it brought a negative outcome. It's the same thing with those kids. It might feel cool to hang out with them, but what is the outcome going to be?"

"I know it'll be negative," Jemal's brother said. "But it's hard to wait for something better when you can have something good right now."

"I know," said Jemal, "but would you rather have the smaller problem of waiting or the bigger problem of the negative outcome? Positive decisions get positive outcomes, and you can feel good about yourself too. Negative decisions not only bring negative outcomes but also make you end up feeling bad about yourself. You deserve better than that—think about making choices that will make your life better, not worse."

try this

For each situation, write one possible positive decision and one possible negative decision and tell what the outcome would be for each.

Julia is buying only one candy bar, but she has to stand in a long line to pay for it. She doesn't have much time. She thinks about just putting it in her pocket and walking out.

Possible positive decision: _____

Outcome: _____

Possible negative decision: _____

Outcome: _____

Rick always wishes that Zach would talk to him because Zach is really popular. One day Zach asks Rick to cheat for him on an upcoming test.

Possible positive decision: _____

Outcome: _____

Possible negative decision: _____

Outcome: _____

Chloe's date wants her to be more intimate than she wants to be. She's afraid the relationship might end if she doesn't agree.

Possible positive decision: _____

Outcome: _____

Possible negative decision: _____

Outcome: _____

Brandon learns some personal information about a student no one likes. He knows that sharing the information would make him look cool.

Possible positive decision: _____

Outcome: _____

Possible negative decision: _____

Outcome: _____

Anya's uncle is in the hospital with a terminal illness. She was planning to go with her family to visit him. Then she was invited to the best party of the year on the same day.

Possible positive decision: _____

Outcome: _____

Possible negative decision: _____

Outcome: _____

now try this

Observe and record decisions you or others make throughout the day. Next to each, circle the plus sign if you think it is a positive decision and the minus sign if you think it is a negative decision, and tell why. At http://www.newharbinger.com/50003, you can download a form to use for this exercise.

$+ -$ 1. _____

_____

Because: _____

_____

$+ -$ 2. _____

_____

Because: _____

_____

$+ -$ 3. _____

_____

Because: _____

_____

+ — 4. _____

_____

Because: _____

_____

+ — 5. _____

_____

Because: _____

_____

Explain a positive decision you once made and describe its outcome.

_____

_____

_____

_____

_____

_____

How was your self-esteem affected by this outcome?

_____

Explain a negative decision you once made and describe its outcome.

_____

_____

_____

_____

_____

_____

How was your self-esteem affected by this outcome?

_____

Imagine and describe a world where everyone made only positive decisions. What would be different or the same?

_____

_____

_____

_____

today's affirmation

Making positive decisions will bring me positive outcomes.

42 the power of facing challenges head-on

know this

When a situation looks difficult, you might want to ignore it, avoid it, or make it go away. But when we don't face challenges head-on, we end up making things worse. Facing challenges helps us feel better about ourselves and creates healthy self-esteem.

Sydney was given a detention slip for getting to class late. She was supposed to take it home, have it signed by her parents, and then stay an hour after school on Friday. Sydney knew her parents would ground her. They'd been on her for everything lately, and this was going to make things worse. As she was walking to the bus, the detention slip fell out of her books and onto the ground. Sydney hesitated. Instead of picking it up, she watched the wind whisk it away. Sydney smiled. That takes care of that problem, *she thought.*

On Monday morning, Sydney's father got a call from the vice principal. Sydney now had a second detention for not showing up for the first. One more and she could be suspended. Sydney's parents grounded her for two weeks—one for getting a detention in the first place, the second for not telling them, which they called a "lie of omission."

Sydney is trying to make problems go away by avoiding them. But instead of getting rid of one problem, she has created another on top of the first. When we don't face challenges head-on, we make things worse.

try this

Tell what additional problem might arise because of these kids not facing their challenges head-on.

Tracy felt so nervous around other kids that she would throw up in the girls' bathroom before school. But she wouldn't talk to the counselor her mom had found for her.

_____

_____

Rob scratched his dad's car door by running into it with his bike. He tried to cover up the scratch with dirt.

_____

_____

Amanda didn't understand the math homework, so she skipped math class on the day of the test.

_____

_____

Joe wasn't going to get home by curfew and he knew his parents would be mad, so he stayed out all night to avoid them.

_____

_____

Michelle got bad headaches after her grandfather died. She didn't want to go to the doctor, so she didn't tell her mother.

_____

_____

now try this

Circle the phrases that describe things you have done, or seen other people do, to avoid facing challenges head-on. Use the blank lines to add your own.

eat too much	take drugs	stay on devices too long
drink alcohol	isolate myself	run away
sleep too much	stay home	hurt myself
watch too much TV	overexercise	stop eating
work too much	be overinvolved in activities	_____
avoid someone or something	blame others	_____
lie	deny a problem	_____
		_____

Describe a challenge you are dealing with that feels difficult to face.

_____

_____

_____

_____

Tell what would happen if you avoided it by using one of the behaviors listed above.

_____

_____

_____

_____

Tell how your self-esteem would be affected if you did this.

_____

_____

_____

_____

Tell what would happen if you faced this challenge head-on.

_____

_____

_____

_____

Tell how your self-esteem would be affected if you did this.

_____

_____

_____

_____

today's affirmation

Facing my challenges is the only way to solve them and
helps create healthy self–esteem.

43 setting realistic goals

Sometimes we have trouble achieving goals because we set them too high. For example, we might think, *I'm going to turn my life around. This semester I'll join three clubs, learn to play an instrument, get a part-time job, and change my grades from Ds to straight As.* Or we might think, *I really want to get into better physical shape by running. I'm going to sign up for the marathon in two weeks.*

For most people, either of these goals would be unrealistic and cause too much physical and emotional pressure. Most of us would run out of energy and quit trying early on. We have a better chance of achieving bigger goals if we set them as long-term goals—something to accomplish over a longer period of time. Then we can set realistic short-term goals as steps toward our long-term goals. For example, the short-term goals of joining one club, deciding what instrument to play, applying for a job, and spending more time on homework and test preparation are realistic steps toward reaching the longer-term goal of turning our life around. The short-term goal of starting to run three times a week is a realistic step toward getting into better physical shape and someday running a marathon.

Knowing how to set realistic short- and long-term goals can help us create more successes and healthier self-esteem.

try this

A short-term goal is one to be achieved in the near future (such as passing tomorrow's test); a long-term goal is one to be achieved in the more distant future (such as graduating from college.) Short- and long-term goals are relative to a person's age and situation.

For each of these statements, circle S if you think it would work best as a short-term goal and L if it would work best as a long-term goal.

S L   speak Spanish fluently

S L   fill out a job application

S L   go to PE class

S L   win a surfing competition

S L   watch a lacrosse match to see how it's played

S L   sign up for Spanish I

S L   work as a camp counselor

S L   go surfing for an hour each day

S L   raise your PE grade

S L   be the highest scorer on the lacrosse team

Write three to five short-term goals that would lead toward each of the following kids' long-term goals.

As a freshman, Arianna hopes to sing a solo in the school chorus one day.

1. _____

2. _____

3. _____

4. _____

5. _____

Cho wants to upgrade his phone but needs money to pay for it.

1. _____
2. _____
3. _____
4. _____
5. _____

Christopher wants to get an article published in the school newspaper.

1. _____
2. _____
3. _____
4. _____
5. _____

Dyanna wants to go to the dance with Charlie but she has never actually met him.

1. _____
2. _____
3. _____
4. _____
5. _____

now try this

At the top of each ladder, write one long-term goal you would like to accomplish in the next six months. On each rung, write one short-term goal leading toward the long-term goal at the top of that ladder. Add more rungs if necessary.

My Long-Term Goal

My Long-Term Goal

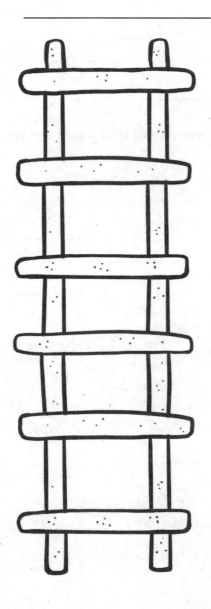
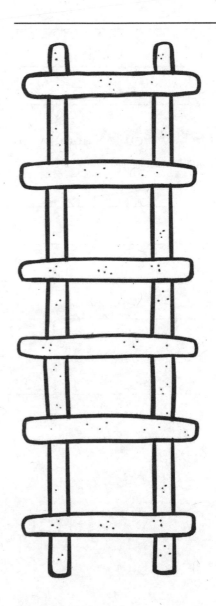

Describe how you feel about yourself when you set your sights too high and then don't achieve your goal.

_____

_____

_____

_____

_____

Describe how you feel about yourself when you achieve a goal that you have wanted for a long time.

_____

_____

_____

_____

_____

_____

today's affirmation

I think realistically to achieve my goals.

Dev felt down on himself a lot. There was always something that felt hard for him to handle. Class assignments were complicated; relationships were complicated; his job was complicated. When one thing cleared up, something else went wrong; it never seemed to stop. Dev shared his frustration with his school counselor, Ms. Nash. She explained that most all of our problems can be solved, but Dev said he never knew where or how to start.

Ms. Nash wrote down six steps Dev could take to help him solve problems. She explained each one, using Dev's first challenge, "Class assignments are complicated," as an example.

Step 1: Take a breath and clear your mind.

Beginning from a center of calm helps us think better!

Step 2: Clearly define the problem.

We have a better chance of changing something when we know exactly what needs to change. Instead of just saying "Class assignments are complicated," Dev could think more about what made them difficult.

Dev said he never felt he understood the assignments clearly. After he turned them in, the teacher often said he hadn't followed the directions. Ms. Nash then defined the problem more clearly by writing: "Have trouble understanding exactly what the teacher wants."

Step 3: Brainstorm solutions.

Next Ms. Nash asked Dev to list all the possible solutions he could think of to that problem, no matter how crazy or far-fetched they sounded. Dev came up with these ideas:

Listen more carefully when the assignment is explained.

Ask a friend to re-explain it to me after class.

Use my phone to record the teacher's explanation of the assignment.

Ask if I can have a different teacher.

Talk with the teacher to see if I understand the assignment correctly before I start.

Drop out of school so I don't have to do homework at all.

Sit closer to the front of the classroom.

Step 4: Choose one solution and try it.

Dev and Ms. Nash went over every item on the list and Dev decided to try "Ask a friend to re-explain it to me after class."

Step 5: Evaluate how well it worked.

Dev tried this plan the next time he got an assignment, but he still didn't do very well. He realized that he wasn't confident his friend had understood what the teacher wanted either.

Step 6: If it worked well, keep doing it. If not, try another solution from the list.

Dev decided to try another idea: "Talk with the teacher to see if I understand the assignment correctly before I start." He did this the next day, and he ended up getting a much better grade on his homework.

As Dev used this method with other challenges in his life, he found that having a plan and some practiced skills made him more confident in his ability to solve problems. This contributed to healthier self-esteem.

try this

You may have more experience with problem solving than you realize; most of us problem solve in many ways every day. A few problem-solving activities are listed below. Circle any that you already know how to do. Then write some more of your own.

planning a party   playing your favorite game

cleaning your room   _____

organizing friends to go to the movies   _____

making your lunch   _____

sharing a picture on your phone   _____

No matter how simple they seem, all these activities involve thinking clearly and making and following a step-by-step plan. Choose two of the activities above and list the problem-solving steps you would use to complete them. (These steps may be similar to or different from the six steps from Dev's counselor.)

_____   _____

_____   _____

_____   _____

_____   _____

_____   _____

_____   _____

Sometimes we underestimate our ability to problem solve in more complicated situations. Think back to bigger problems you've already encountered and solved in the past. These might have to do with school, home, relationships, or activities. Make a list of your successes here.

_____

_____

_____

_____

_____

Describe a situation that happened to you recently that made your self-esteem dip. Tell what steps in a problem-solving plan you could have followed that would have helped you feel better about yourself.

_____

_____

_____

_____

_____

_____

now try this

For this exercise, you may want to download the worksheet at http://www. newharbinger.com/50003 so you'll have plenty of space for brainstorming.

Name a problem you've been facing lately.

_____

Write a clear and concise definition of the problem so you know exactly what you need to work on.

_____

_____

Brainstorm possible solutions to the problem. (For brainstorming to be most effective, it's important that you write down all the ideas that come into your head—without judging them. It doesn't matter how unusual or impossible they may be; write them down anyway.) Make your list as long as possible. If you need more space, use additional paper.

_____   _____

_____   _____

_____   _____

_____   _____

_____   _____

Look back over your list. Now think about which ideas are possible or realistic and which aren't. Choose one of your realistic ideas to try as a solution and write it here. Tell when you plan to try this solution.

_____

After you've tried this idea, describe how well it worked. Has this solution solved the problem?

_____

_____

_____

If this idea didn't work, choose another solution from your list and try that. Describe your results here. Continue trying solutions until you find one that works.

_____

_____

Sometimes a situation will be so complicated or difficult you won't be able to handle it by yourself. In those cases, part of your problem-solving plan should be to find someone to help you. Describe a situation you might encounter in which you would need to ask for help. Tell who you would find to help you.

_____

_____

today's affirmation

I can handle problems by thinking clearly and trying different solutions until I find the one that works best.

---

know this

Sometimes it can feel like we've made so many mistakes or negative choices that we're stuck on a downward path and there's no turning back. But the truth is it's never too late to turn things around in some way. At every moment we're given the chance to start fresh and try again. No matter what has happened, you can always make the decision to move up from where you are instead of continuing to spiral down. When you do, you turn your self-esteem around as well.

Kayla believed she'd been in trouble her whole life. Her parents called her their "difficult" child. As a toddler she "got into things," and as a teen she was grounded repeatedly for making poor choices. She had shoplifted, taken her parents' car before she had a permit, and been caught smoking and suspended from school twice. She pretended she didn't care but really she felt terrible. Kayla told her counselor, Erica, how much she hated herself and her life. When Erica asked if she'd like to change, Kayla said, "Of course, but I can't. I'm just bad." Erica told her that no one is "just bad," no matter what they've done, and that her past didn't determine her future; only she did. She taught Kayla how to relax, open her mind, and think about consequences before acting. Kayla practiced recognizing her choices and making positive decisions. The more positive outcomes she got, the more she believed that she could change. Over the next year she turned around both her life and her self-esteem.

Gage and Kevin were riding in Harry's car on a warm summer night. They thought it would be funny to throw water balloons at some kids they knew and laughed when they got wet. But then a water balloon hit the windshield of a passing car, causing the driver to swerve and almost hit a tree. He called the police, and the boys had to appear in court and perform community service for three months. The judge spoke clearly: "Turn it around. Change this problem into an opportunity. Don't let these circumstances limit you." The boys worked as mentors to younger kids who were in trouble. They helped them with homework and sports, and just hung out together. The younger kids started looking up to the three boys and it felt good. After three months the judge commended the boys and said the volunteer agency was offering them part-time jobs as activity leaders.

try this

Turning things around takes energy, but staying on a negative path makes things worse. Identify possible positive changes you could make by answering these questions:

List any life situations you'd like to turn around and tell why.

_____

_____

_____

_____

_____

Describe any habits you'd like to turn around. Tell how this could have a positive effect on your life.

_____

_____

_____

_____

_____

Explain how these current situations and habits affect your self-esteem.

_____

_____

_____

Describe any way you'd like to turn your self-esteem around.

_____

_____

_____

_____

Identify the thoughts and feelings that come up when you think about turning things around.

_____

_____

_____

_____

_____

_____

now try this

The following list describes actions that can help people turn things around. Circle any you think you'd feel comfortable doing. Add more of your own.

apologize   try a new way of behaving

make amends   do something nice for someone

create positive thoughts   give love

forgive   believe in yourself

admit your part in the problem   _____

pay the consequences and move on   _____

clean up what you messed up   _____

ask for help   _____

Identify one turnaround you'd like to start working on.

_____

Put a star next to any actions from the above list that you could use to create a plan for change.

Your turnaround is a long-term goal. Set some realistic short-term goals for working toward your long-term goal.

_____

_____

_____

Take the first step this week and record what happened here.

_____

_____

_____

Make a plan for when and how you can take further steps toward your goal.

_____

_____

_____

_____

_____

_____

Important Note: If the thought of your turnaround feels overwhelming or impossible to achieve, ask an adult you trust to help you get started, or even see you all the way through. Remember that any discomfort this challenge creates will be far outweighed by how good you'll feel about yourself when you accomplish your goal.

today's affirmation

No matter what I've done in the past, I can always make
the choice to turn things around and get back on track.

46 smart people ask for help

know this

Asking for help doesn't mean you aren't competent. It means you're strong enough and wise enough to recognize when doing something all by yourself would lead to a negative outcome, or that you'll succeed to a far greater extent if you consult with other people. Asking for help when appropriate will bring you more positive outcomes and create healthier self-esteem.

Sometimes we think being capable and mature means handling everything on our own all the time. We don't ask for help because we'd feel humiliated or imagine people would look down on us. In reality, the opposite is true. While it's important to build problem-solving skills for manageable tasks, it's just as important to know when asking for help is the best solution.

In different situations it's more or less critical to ask for help. If you're ever feeling severely depressed, if you're being emotionally or physically abused, or if you're ill or in danger, it's very critical that you reach out to someone who can help you stay safe. If you're having a somewhat bad day, if someone gave you a negative look, or if you've got a paper cut, you can still ask for help but it's probably less critical.

The smartest and most successful people make a habit of asking for help when they need it. The proverb "Two heads are better than one" has stood the test of time because it's true: guidance from those with more experience or knowledge can bring you the right information to move ahead successfully. Learning something new from a teacher, mentor, or friend increases your own knowledge and your chances for success. This helps build healthy self-esteem.

try this

What do you tell yourself about the need to ask someone else for help?

_____

_____

_____

_____

What feelings come up when you think these thoughts?

_____

_____

_____

_____

Think of all the people who've helped you through your life to this point. These might be parents, other family members, teachers, coaches, friends, neighbors, doctors, counselors, or others. Someone helped you up when you were learning to walk; someone steadied you as you learned to balance on a bike; someone explained numbers and counting as you learned to add. Because those people helped you, you were able to achieve your goals and feel good about yourself. No one looked down on you because you needed help with something new.

Make a list of anyone you can remember helping you through your life so far. Next to their name write what they did.

_____

_____

_____

_____

_____

Helping goes two ways. Make a list of anyone you have helped when they needed it. Tell who it was and what you did.

_____

_____

_____

_____

_____

now try this

As a teen and young adult, you're learning even more than ever. If you want to expand and grow and try new things, you'll find more success if you ask for help when you need it. Make a list of any challenges you're facing now where asking for help would be a wise choice. Rate each challenge from 1 (low) to 10 (high) as to how critical is it for you to get help with this.

_____

_____

_____

_____

_____

_____

Now brainstorm a support list of anyone you know and trust who might help you with these projects, or any new people you might approach. On a separate piece of paper or in your phone, write their names and the challenge they can help with. Add the person's phone number or email address and make a plan for when you'll contact that person.

Keep this list for future use as you become more confident in asking for help.

today's affirmation

Asking for help when I need it is a sign of wisdom, not weakness.

conclusion

Congratulations! You've just completed a significant step on the journey to understanding, accepting, and caring for your authentic self to create healthy self-esteem! This is some of the most important life work you will ever do, and you'll realize the benefits more and more as you continue on your journey.

Now take a moment to stop, relax, smile, and reward yourself. You've done a great job!

Lisa M. Schab, LCSW, is a practicing psychotherapist in the greater Chicago, IL, area; and author of eighteen self-help books, including *The Anxiety Workbook for Teens*, and the teen guided journals, *Put Your Worries Here* and *Put Your Feelings Here*. She has been interviewed as an expert on the Milwaukee television stations WTMJ-TV and WISN-TV, and for articles in *The New York Times*, Scholastic's *Choices* magazine, *Teen Vogue*, *Psych Central*, and *Your Teen Magazine*. Schab has authored regular columns on tweens and teens for *Chicago Parent*, and on healthy families for *The Sun Newspapers*. She is a member of the National Association of Social Workers (NASW).

Did you know there are **free tools** you can download for this book?

Free tools are things like **worksheets**, **guided meditation exercises**, and **more** that will help you get the most out of your book.

You can download free tools for this book— whether you bought or borrowed it, in any format, from any source—from the New Harbinger website. All you need is a NewHarbinger.com account. Just use the URL provided in this book to view the free tools that are available for it. Then, click on the "download" button for the free tool you want, and follow the prompts that appear to log in to your NewHarbinger.com account and download the material.

You can also save the free tools for this book to your **Free Tools Library** so you can access them again anytime, just by logging in to your account! Just look for this button on the book's free tools page.

+ Save this to my free tools library

If you need help accessing or downloading free tools, visit **newharbinger.com/faq** or contact us at **customerservice@newharbinger.com**.